Immigrant Entrepreneurship in Sweden

Daniel Rauhut

Immigrant Entrepreneurship in Sweden

Economic Perspectives

palgrave
macmillan

Daniel Rauhut
Department of Economic History
Lund University
Lund, Sweden

ISBN 978-3-032-02465-7 ISBN 978-3-032-02466-4 (eBook)
https://doi.org/10.1007/978-3-032-02466-4

This Palgrave Macmillan imprint is published by the registered company Springer Nature Switzerland AG.
The registered company address is: Gewerbestrasse 11, 6330 Cham, Switzerland

Acknowledgements

As always, there are several people other than the author involved in a book project. I would like to send my thanks to Vivek Sundriyal, Ghazal Zalkat and Neelambar Hatti for their rich, generous, and critically constructive comments on earlier versions of this manuscript. The discussions I have had with Svante Lingärde and Marika Gruber on this topic have enriched the manuscript. Moreover, I would like to thank Francisco Cobos Cabral for producing the maps. The shortcomings that still exist should not be attributed to them; these shortcomings are my responsibility as the author to bear. Lastly, I also want to thank Wyndham Hacket Pain for his help and support during the different stages in the production process, together with the Palgrave Macmillan production team.

Lund, Sweden
March 2025

Daniel Rauhut

Contents

About the Author

Daniel Rauhut is an associate professor with a PhD in Economic History. He is an affiliated researcher at the Department of Economic History, Lund University, Sweden, and at the Centro de Estudos Geográficos, Universidade de Lisboa, Portugal. For over 25 years, he has addressed international migration and immigrant integration at universities in Sweden, Norway, and Finland, participating in numerous EU-funded research projects. His research focuses on EU social policies, labour market integration of immigrants, Swedish emigration to Portugal, and the socio-economic impact of third-country nationals in peripheral regions.He is a peer reviewer for 20 scientific journals, a board member of the Nordic section of the ERSA, and received an international research award in 2017. He co-edited *Poverty in the History of Economic Thought* (Routledge, 2020), *Poverty in Contemporary Economic Thought* (Routledge, 2021), *EU Cohesion Policy and Spatial Governance* (Edward Elgar, 2021), *Assessing the Social Impact of Immigration in Europe: Renegotiating Remoteness* (Edward Elgar, 2023), and *Inequality: Social and Economic Aspects* (Routledge, 2024). Recently, he edited *New Methods and Theory on Immigrant Integration: Insights from Remote and Peripheral Areas* (Edward Elgar, 2023) and co-authored *The Economics of Immigration beyond the Cities: Theoretical Perspectives and Empirical Insights* (Palgrave Macmillan, 2023).

List of Figures

CHAPTER 1

Introduction

Abstract The introductory chapter outlines the background for this essay, presents key literature, and some statistics over the development of immigrant entrepreneurship in Sweden over time, as well as providing a rationale for the study. Moreover, the aim and research questions are explicitly formulated. The introductory chapter ends with a roadmap.

Keywords Immigrant entrepreneurship • Institutions • Integration • Historical migration • Policy implications

1.1 Background

This essay will discuss several disparate areas—immigration, entrepreneurship, and institutions—to explore how they interact and what role they play, and have played historically, in creating wealth and prosperity in Sweden. It is the intersection between these areas this essay will explore. By examining the intersection between immigration, entrepreneurship, and institutions, researchers and policymakers can better understand how to harness the potential of immigrant entrepreneurs, ultimately contributing to more inclusive and prosperous economies. In the literature, five areas where such broader understanding is beneficial are highlighted: (a) *Economic growth and innovation*: Immigrant entrepreneurs significantly contribute to economic growth and innovation. They often bring diverse

D. Rauhut, *Immigrant Entrepreneurship in Sweden*,
https://doi.org/10.1007/978-3-032-02466-4_1

skills, perspectives, and networks that foster new business creation and technological advancements (Nijkamp et al., 2012; Kondoh, 2017; Bodvarsson & Van den Berg, 2013; Bansak et al., 2021). (b) *Institutional influence*: The institutional environment, including legal, economic, and social frameworks, profoundly impacts entrepreneurial activities. Institutions can either facilitate or hinder the entrepreneurial endeavours of immigrants. Understanding these dynamics helps in formulating policies that support immigrant entrepreneurship and, consequently, economic development (Rosenberg & Birdzell Jr, 1986; North & Thomas, 1973; North, 1999; Schön, 2000). (c) *Cultural diversity and competitiveness*: Immigrant entrepreneurs often introduce cultural diversity into the business ecosystem, which can enhance creativity and competitiveness. This diversity can lead to the development of unique products and services, catering to a broader market (Rauhut et al., 2023; Muñoz-Mora et al., 2022). (d) *Risk-taking and resilience*: Immigrants tend to exhibit higher levels of risk-taking and resilience compared to native entrepreneurs. These traits are essential for entrepreneurial success and can lead to more robust and dynamic business environments (Stark, 1991). (e) *Policy implications*: Insights from studying this intersection can inform policymakers on how to create supportive environments for immigrant entrepreneurs. This includes addressing barriers such as access to finance, legal hurdles, and social integration challenges (Borjas, 2019; Chiswick, 2019; Bansak et al., 2021).

In the USA, immigrant entrepreneurs play a pivotal role in driving innovation and economic growth. They are responsible for a significant share of new business creation and patents. The institutional environment, characterised by relatively supportive legal and economic frameworks, facilitates entrepreneurial activities. However, challenges such as access to capital and navigating complex regulatory landscapes persist (Fairlie, 2013). In Europe, the institutional context varies significantly across countries, influencing immigrant entrepreneurship differently. The European Union has implemented various initiatives to support migrant entrepreneurs, such as the EU Guidebook to Promote and Support Migrant Entrepreneurship (CEC, 2016). These efforts aim to address barriers like access to finance, legal hurdles, and social integration.

In Sweden, immigrant entrepreneurship is recognised for its potential to contribute to economic diversity and innovation. However, immigrant entrepreneurs face unique challenges, including the 'liability of newness', which refers to the difficulties new businesses encounter in establishing themselves (Zalkat, 2024; Klinthäll et al., 2016). Swedish institutions and authorities play a crucial role in either facilitating or hindering entrepreneurial activities. Research indicates that immigrant entrepreneurs in Sweden often rely on ethnic networks and niche markets to overcome these challenges (Gruber & Rauhut, 2024; Miao, 2020; Ohlsson et al., 2012).

1.2 Immigration

Even during the Middle Ages, Sweden was a country of immigration. Immigrants primarily came from the German territories, from Finland (which at that time was part of Sweden), but also from the Baltic region. These were invited merchants with substantial wealth and networks. Additionally, craftsmen, soldiers, and servants sought their way to Sweden. During the sixteenth century, immigrants from the German territories and Finland continued to dominate immigration to Sweden. Under King Gustav Vasa, Sweden began to consciously recruit skilled foreigners. This included doctors, builders, masons, carpenters, joiners, blacksmiths, tinsmiths, gunsmiths, goldsmiths, tailors, saddlers, glovemakers, brewers, printers. Many of them came from England, Poland, the Baltic region, and France. Shipbuilders and sailmakers came from the Netherlands. Specialists in the mining industry were mainly imported from the German territories. During the era of the Swedish Empire, merchants with substantial wealth and networks continued to be recruited, as well as architects and builders from Italy and the Netherlands (Svanberg & Tydén, 1992). Although it is not evident in the scant literature available, it is reasonable to assume that many of these immigrants started small businesses which they operated in Sweden.

The era of the Swedish Empire also marked Sweden's transformation into a cosmopolitan country, with immigration from all parts of the realm. Additionally, there was immigration from countries such as Denmark, the German territories, the Netherlands, Wallonia, Flanders, and France. Simultaneously, a royal decree was issued in 1685 expelling Jews from Sweden. Following the end of the Swedish Empire with the death of King Karl XII in 1718 and the subsequent Great Nordic War (1720–1721), immigration to Sweden decreased, and national diversity diminished. At the same time, the immigration of wealthy merchants and entrepreneurs from Scotland, the Netherlands, England, and the German territories increased. Under King Gustav III, French culture became fashionable in Sweden. The immigration ban on Catholics and Jews was lifted in the 1770s (Svanberg & Tydén, 1992).

From the 1860s until the 1930s, Sweden was a country of emigration. Young, healthy individuals left Sweden in search of a better life, primarily in North America (Lundh & Ohlsson, 1994a). Although Sweden experienced net emigration during this period, efforts were made to attract skilled workers in shortage occupations (Svanberg & Tydén, 1992). The first waves of refugees also began arriving in Sweden towards the end of the nineteenth century. These were mainly Eastern European Jews fleeing pogroms in Tsarist Russia (Nordlund, 1999). During and after World War II, larger and more numerous waves of refugees arrived in Sweden, primarily from countries close to Sweden (Svanberg & Tydén, 1992).

In the late 1940s, there was a significant labour shortage in Sweden, prompting the Swedish government to organise the transfer of labour from neighbouring countries to Sweden. The Nordic Council was established in 1952, and one of its primary objectives was to facilitate the movement of labour to work in another Nordic country, implicitly Sweden (Fischer & Straubhaar, 1996). Concurrently, the Swedish government transferred German refugees from Eastern Europe, who had been gathered in camps in the occupation zones in West Germany and Austria controlled by the USA, the United Kingdom, and France (Tempsch, 1997). Approximately 25 percent of all immigrants who came to Sweden between 1945 and 1970 were refugees (Rauhut, 2014).

In the early 1970s, labour immigration to Sweden began to decline. One reason for this was the stagnation of Swedish industry, which no longer required foreign labour. Instead, non-European refugee flows began to increase during the 1970s. Political refugees from South America and Asia started arriving, as did refugees from the turbulent Middle East. The Yugoslav civil war created a new wave of European refugees in the early 1990s (Lundh & Ohlsson, 1994a). During the first two decades of the twenty-first century, non-European refugee immigration continued to rise, peaking during the so-called refugee crisis in 2015 (Laine & Rauhut, 2018). Russia's unprovoked war against Ukraine in 2022 generated a larger wave of refugees within Europe than the post-World War II refugee wave (Rauhut et al., 2022).

1.3 Immigrant Entrepreneurship

While research on immigrant entrepreneurship and immigrant entrepreneurs is extensive in countries such as the USA (Fairlie & Lofstrom, 2013; Dabić et al., 2020), the corresponding research in Sweden is relatively narrow and fragmented in nature (Klinthäll et al., 2016; Ekberg & Hammarstedt, 1999). In fact, it took until the mid-1980s until Swedish research realised that there was immigrant entrepreneurship in Sweden (Nordlund, 1999). The increasing refugee flows to Sweden during the 1980s and 1990s (Svanberg & Tydén, 1992; Lundh & Ohlsson, 1994a), as well as an increasing unemployment among immigrants made immigrants and their precarious and troublesome labour market situation more visible (Lundh & Ohlsson, 1994b). Immigrant entrepreneurship had for a long time been hidden by industry's high demand for labour, but as industry demanded less immigrant labour, the existence of immigrant entrepreneurship was uncovered (Nordlund, 1999).

Since the late 1990s the research on immigrants in Sweden has produced numerous studies to explain the lack of integration, mostly on the gap between natives and immigrants regarding employment, unemployment, incomes etc. The focus is on why immigrants are different. While the economics-oriented research points at a significantly lower human capital and lower educational attainment levels, and low language proficiency to explain this gap,[1] the research done in social sciences has pointed at a structural discrimination of immigrants on the Swedish labour market.[2]

The research on immigrant entrepreneurship in Sweden exists but is not as extensive as the research on labour market integration. Recent research on immigrant entrepreneurship in Sweden has largely been fragmented with a focus on topics such as family ties (e.g., Evansluong &

[1] The overviews by e.g., Lundh et al. (2002), Åslund et al. (2006) and Nordström Skans and Åslund (2009) identify poor language proficiency as key problems for many immigrants to enter the Swedish labour market. Studies by e.g., Ekelund and Larsson (2023) and Rauhut et al. (2023) point at the low educational attainment level for many of the refugee groups coming to Sweden. Significant educational investments are needed to make these immigrants competitive at the Swedish labour market.

[2] Studies by e.g., Bask (2005), Aldén and Hammarstedt (2016), Groglopo et al. (2023), Bentsen (2022), Lundborg and Skedinger (2016), Bevelander (1999, 2010), Khosravi (2012), Hällsten et al. (2013), Dahlstedt and Hertzberg (2007), Bursell (2014), Åslund and Rooth (2005), Gustafsson and Zheng (2006), Kamali (2016), Adman and Jansson (2017), Macuchova and Rauhut (2023) and Behtoui et al. (2019) discuss this.

Ramírez-Pasillas, 2019), embeddedness (e.g., Tavassoli & Trippl, 2019), or focused on a particular sector (e.g., Barth & Zalkat, 2021). The spatial dimension of immigrant entrepreneurship has been discussed in some publications (Andersson & Hammarstedt, 2015; Andersson & Larsson, 2016; Rauhut & Rauhut Kompaniets, 2018; Andersson et al., 2021).

One of the most comprehensive overviews on immigrant entrepreneurship in Sweden is an appendix to a public commission report by the Ministry of Cultural Affairs in 1999 (Nordlund, 1999). In a way, it is significant for the research on immigrant entrepreneurship that it reduces the study object to a cultural question. It is also deplorable to note that no overview studies of this research area in Sweden have been done in the last 25 years. The popular science book by Anders Johnson (2010) can also be mentioned here. It is an overview of all successful companies founded by immigrants in Sweden. Why immigrants started companies, where etc. are not accounted for, just the successful ones are discussed. The book is published by a neoliberal think-tank and the key message is that with less regulations more immigrants would start successful companies. However, the volume struggles with significant problems. One, and perhaps the most pertinent, problem is that the impact of the 1864 Business Freedom Ordinance is overlooked (which was removed in the late 1960s). According to this regulation, immigrant companies were e.g., not allowed to compete with companies run by natives nor contravene with Swedish business practice, and the immigrant had to show security for three years' taxes to the state and municipality. As few immigrants could meet these requirements, they had to wait to start a company until they became Swedish citizens (it took at least ten years to become a Swedish citizen) or start the company in partnership with a native. In both cases, it is possible to argue that these companies cannot be considered as immigrant companies, or, at least, that they do not meet the criteria we have today when talking about immigrant entrepreneurship.

An overview study of immigrant entrepreneurship in the Netherlands states that the social scientists analysing this research area reduce immigrant entrepreneurship to an ethnocultural phenomenon existing within an economic and institutional vacuum, focussing on structural changes in the urban economy and the institutional framework of the welfare state within which entrepreneurs operate (Rath & Kloostermann, 2000). Similar arguments have been raised in Swedish studies (Kazlou & Urban, 2023). However, similar to the Dutch context, Swedish studies have often overlooked the broader institutional and economic frameworks within which immigrant entrepreneurship operates. This comparison highlights the universal challenge of moving beyond ethnocultural reductionism in this field.

Given this fragmented research landscape, a more nuanced understanding of immigrant entrepreneurship in Sweden is needed to inform policy and practice. This historical and economic overview underscores the need for more comprehensive studies that move beyond fragmented and culturally reductive approaches. Future research should address the intersection of economic, historical, and institutional dimensions to fully understand the dynamics of immigrant entrepreneurship in Sweden.

1.4 Institutions and Institutional Change

Understanding the interplay between formal and informal institutions is essential for effective integration policies as well as stimulating immigrant entrepreneurship. Distinguishing between formal and informal institutions is common, but the exact distinction varies. 'Formal' typically refers to explicit, written rules enforced by the state, while 'informal' rules remain implicit (Kingston & Caballero, 2009). Milgrom et al. (1990) argue that specialised actors enforce formal rules, while relevant group members enforce informal codes of behaviour. North (1991) defines informal constraints as 'codes of conduct, norms of behaviour, and conventions', including extensions and modifications of formal rules. These informal institutions are part of our cultural heritage.

In the context of immigrant entrepreneurship, institutions—both formal and informal—play a crucial role. North (1991, 1999) views institutions as the 'rules of the game' in society, shaping human interaction and reducing uncertainty in everyday life. These institutions encompass formal laws and constitutions as well as unwritten conventions and norms (March & Olsen, 1986, 1989). Economics and entrepreneurship depend on human beliefs and values, on norms and, also, social hierarchy (Searle, 2005). Regarding immigrant entrepreneurship, institutions determine how natives perceive immigrants, immigrant entrepreneurship, and immigrant entrepreneurs. Informal institutions influence both immigrants and natives, affecting the process of coexistence, enrichment, and adaptation. They define who belongs and how much immigrants assimilate into the new culture (Rauhut, 2020).

When relative prices shift, parties engaged in an exchange (whether political or economic) may recognise the potential for improved outcomes through altered agreements or contracts. Renegotiation is attempted, but the nested nature of contracts within a rule hierarchy can hinder this process. In such cases, parties seeking better bargaining positions may invest resources in restructuring higher-level rules. Additionally, changes in norms due to shifting prices or tastes can gradually replace existing norms over time (North, 1991, 1999). Old rules are eliminated because new interests have grown stronger. In practice, the limitations set by these rules have already been exceeded without the need for any formal institutional changes. When legislation does eventually change, it reflects that power dynamics and practices have already shifted. Consequently, the modification of the formal regulatory framework is largely of an *ex-post* nature. By aligning practice with formal rules, the forces from more advanced positions can remove remaining obstacles to new development (Schön, 2000).

This brief theoretical discussion on institutions and their role in immigrant entrepreneurship leads to the conclusion that immigrant entrepreneurship is a function of both formal and informal institutions. This is not a novelty. When formal institutions change, the change reflects a change in the informal institutions, i.e., in the norms, values and preferences of the population as well as political and economic actors. When the regulations change for immigrant entrepreneurship, or entrepreneurship for some specific immigrant groups, it reflects that those in control of the regulatory formal institutions expect to profit from a changed legal framework.

1.5 Theoretical Approaches

The theoretical approaches used to explain immigrant entrepreneurship in Sweden are the same as the one in the international research. One marked difference is that the New Economics of Migration theory, with its prediction on immigrant entrepreneurship, has not attracted many scholars in Sweden. This is an interesting observation as the theory appears to have an explanatory potential on the immigrant entrepreneurship in Sweden.[3]

In *neoclassical economics*, self-employment is a significant aspect of employment opportunities for immigrant labour. Immigrants are more likely to be self-employed compared to natives with similar skills. Borjas (1986) finds that the probability of self-employment increases for immigrants the longer they reside in the destination country. Immigrants often

[3] To the best of my knowledge, I have not heard about any study on immigrant entrepreneurship in Sweden based on the New Economics of Migration theory.

face unemployment and may be forced to take jobs below their formal qualifications (Chiswick & Miller, 2010). Geographic enclaves also provide opportunities for self-employment among individuals with similar national or ethnic backgrounds (Borjas, 2003). Immigrants exhibit higher entrepreneurial activity than natives, creating new jobs and benefits for the native population (Simon, 2002).

The New Economics of Migration theory also supports this view, suggesting that immigrants are more likely to start businesses than natives. This tendency is not necessarily due to greater entrepreneurial spirit but rather the need to create better conditions for themselves in a new country. Immigrants often struggle to signal their productivity to employers, resulting in a marginal position in the labour market (Stark, 1991). There is a self-selection among labour immigrants: they are typically young, willing to take risks, more assertive, and may possess top competence in niche areas. The businesses they start are often labour-intensive and require minimal investment capital.

In the Marxist labour theory of value, the exchange value of an object is determined by the amount of labour required on average to produce it. The capitalist thus extracts more value (produced goods) from the worker than he gets back in return for the work (wages). The consequence is that the worker is exploited (Sweezy, 1970). This is particularly true of immigrant labour (Piore, 1979). It is in the interest of the capitalist system to have a reserve army of cheap labour (Sweezy, 1970). In the Marxist-inspired *dual labour market theory*, immigrant labour is essential to meet the demand for unskilled workers in the capitalist production system. Immigrants are expected to remain as wage labourers rather than becoming entrepreneurs. Consequently, the destination country may attempt to hinder immigrants' ambitions to become entrepreneurs and self-employed (Piore, 1979; Morokvasic, 1984; Kofman, 1999).[4] In accordance with this kind of reasoning, it is therefore logical that some research on immigrant entrepreneurship points precisely to the fact that the immigrant

[4] Postcolonialism and whiteness studies develop the Marxist arguments and apply them to immigrant populations in today's developed economies. Non-white people are subjected to structural violence by whites and the consequence is that the non-whites are discriminated against and exploited. The same logic is advanced by postcolonialism: the colonised peoples are subjected to structural violence by the colonising peoples, and this continues even today in the former colonial powers against the population with roots in the former colonised countries. The root cause of the structural violence is the capitalist production system (Rauhut & Laine, 2023).

entrepreneurs are exposed to structural violence, that they are exploited and subjected to discrimination, by financiers, by customers, etc. (see Ålund, 2000; Behtoui, 2004; Brundin et al., 2001; Dahlstedt & Hertzberg, 2005; de los Reyes et al., 2002; Knocke & Hertzberg, 2000; Magnusson, 2001; Muhr, 2020; Neergaard, 2002; Pripp, 2001; Sawyer, 2006; Slavnic, 2008, 2013; Tovatt, 2016).

1.6 What This Book Is About

This essay discusses immigrant entrepreneurship in Sweden from an economic and historical perspective. Although this overview begins in the Middle Ages, the emphasis is on the last 60 years. The key questions this essay will discuss are (1) in what sectors and industry immigrant entrepreneurship has taken place, (2) why it has taken place, (3) where it has taken place geographically, and (4) what its economic and social impact have been. The essay will also try to answer (5) to what extent the development of immigrant entrepreneurship in Sweden is unique for Sweden or has followed international trends. Unlike previous studies, this essay seeks to provide a holistic analysis by integrating historical, economic, and spatial perspectives while addressing the institutional and regulatory factors that have shaped immigrant entrepreneurship in Sweden.

The essay starts with a methodological chapter defining key concepts, limitation etc., followed by a chapter discussing immigrant entrepreneurship in different periods over time. Then the focus is turned to the geographical distribution of immigrant entrepreneurship over time, its economic and social consequences as well as the key institutional changes over time. After this, questions related to how the Swedish scholarship on immigrant entrepreneurship is discussed, e.g., the context of immigrant entrepreneurship, and the research focus in Sweden on immigrant entrepreneurship. A discussion on policy aspects related to immigrant entrepreneurship in Sweden and to what extent the immigrant entrepreneurship represents a potential Swedish 'Sonderweg' precedes the discussion and concluding remarks.

The added value of this essay is multifaceted, contributing significantly both scientifically and policy-wise. Scientifically, this essay provides a comprehensive historical analysis, tracing the evolution of support for immigrant entrepreneurs from the Middle Ages through to modern times. It enriches the literature on institutional frameworks, highlighting how legal, economic, and social institutions shape opportunities and barriers for immigrants. Introducing the concept of path dependency in the context of immigrant entrepreneurship, the study offers a novel perspective on how historical exclusionary practices create enduring barriers. Moreover, it calls for a clearer definition of immigrant entrepreneurship, emphasising the need to distinguish between different forms of entrepreneurial activities and their unique challenges.

From a policy perspective, the findings underscore the necessity for equitable support mechanisms to immigrant entrepreneurs, particularly those starting small businesses. This insight could inform the design of more inclusive economic policies. The essay advocates for comprehensive strategies that address legal, economic, social, and cultural dimensions to support immigrant entrepreneurship, guiding policymakers in creating a supportive environment that fosters economic growth and social integration. Identifying specific institutional barriers needing reform, such as discriminatory regulations and limited access to financial resources, the study provides insights that can shape policy reforms aimed at removing these barriers.

Overall, this study provides valuable insights that can inform both academic research and policy design, ultimately contributing to a more inclusive and supportive environment for immigrant entrepreneurs.

References

Adman, P., & Jansson, H. (2017). A field experiment on ethnic discrimination among local Swedish public officials. *Local Government Studies, 43*(1), 44–63.

Aldén, L., & Hammarstedt, M. (2016). Discrimination in the credit market? Access to financial capital among self-employed immigrants. *Kyklos, 69*(1), 3–31.

Ålund, A. (2000). Etnicitetens mångfald och mångfaldens etniciteter. In E. Olsson (Ed.), *Etnicitetens gränser och mångfald* (pp. 27–79). Carlssons bokförlag.

Andersson, L., & Hammarstedt, M. (2015). Ethnic enclaves, networks and self-employment among Middle Eastern immigrants in Sweden. *International Migration, 53*(6), 27–40.

Andersson, M., & Larsson, J. P. (2016). Local entrepreneurship clusters in cities. *Journal of Economic Geography, 16*(1), 39–66.

Andersson, M., Larsson, J. P., & Öner, Ö. (2021). Ethnic enclaves and self-employment among Middle Eastern immigrants in Sweden: Ethnic capital or enclave size? *Regional Studies, 55*(4), 590–604.

Åslund, O., & Rooth, D. O. (2005). Shifts in attitudes and labor market discrimination: Swedish experiences after 9–11. *Journal of Population Economics, 18*, 603–629.

Åslund, O., Erikson, R., Nordström Skans, O., & Sjögren, A. (2006). *Fritt inträde? Ungdomars och invandrares väg till det första arbetet*. SNS förlag.

Bansak, C., Simpson, N., & Zavodny, M. (2021). *The economics of immigration*. Routledge.

Barth, H., & Zalkat, G. (2021). Refugee entrepreneurship in the agri-food industry: The Swedish experience. *Journal of Rural Studies, 86*, 189–197.

Bask, M. (2005). Welfare problems and social exclusion among immigrants in Sweden. *European Sociological Review, 21*(1), 73–89.

Behtoui, A. (2004). Unequal opportunities for young people with immigrant background in the Swedish labour market. *Labour: Review of Labour Economics and Industrial Relations, 18*(6), 633–660.

Behtoui, A., Hertzberg, F., Jonsson, R., León Rosales, R., & Neergaard, A. (2019). Sweden: The otherization of the descendants of immigrants. In P. A. J. Stevens & A. G. Dworkin (Eds.), *The Palgrave handbook of race and ethnic inequalities in education* (pp. 999–1034). Palgrave Macmillan.

Bentsen, B. M. A. (2022). Intergroup contact and negative attitudes towards immigrants among youth in Sweden: Individual and contextual factors. *Journal of International Migration and Integration, 23*(1), 243–266.

Bevelander, P. (1999). The employment integration of immigrants in Sweden. *Journal of Ethnic and Migration Studies, 25*(3), 445–468.

Bevelander, P. (2010). The immigration and integration experience: The case of Sweden. In U. A. Segal, D. Elliott, & N. S. Mayadas (Eds.), *Immigration worldwide: Policies, practices, and trends* (pp. 286–302). Oxford University Press.

Bodvarsson, Ö. B., & Van den Berg, H. (2013). *The economics of immigration. Theory and policy*. Springer.

Borjas, G. J. (1986). The self-employment experience of immigrants. *Journal of Human Resources, 21*(4), 485–506.

Borjas, G. J. (2003). The labor demand curve is downward sloping: Reexamining the impact of immigration on the labour market. *Quarterly Journal of Economics, 118*(4), 1335–1374.

Borjas, G. J. (2019). Reflections on immigration economics. In B. Elsner (Ed.), *Foundations of migration economics* (pp. 574–582). Oxford University Press.

Brundin, E., Bögenhold, D., & Sundin, E. (2001). Invandrares företagande—Fakta och implikationer. In A. Rosing, C. Råberg, & E. Sundin (red.), *Marginalisering eller integration: Invandrares företagande i svensk retorik och praktik: En forskarantologi* (pp. 61–78). Nutek.

Bursell, M. (2014). The multiple burdens of foreign-named men—Evidence from a field experiment on gendered ethnic hiring discrimination in Sweden. *European Sociological Review, 30*(3), 399–409.

CEC. (2016). *EU guidebook to promote and support migrant entrepreneurship*. Retrieved October 1, 2024, from https://migrant-integration.ec.europa.eu/library-document/eu-guidebook-promote-and-support-migrant-entrepreneurship_en

Chiswick, B. R. (2019). Managing immigration in the 21st century. In B. Elsner (Ed.), *Foundations of migration economics* (pp. 583–595). Oxford University Press.
Chiswick, B. R., & Miller, P. W. (2010). Educational mismatch: Are highly skilled immigrants really working at high-skilled jobs and what Price do they pay if not? In B. R. Chiswick (Ed.), *High skilled immigration in a global labour market* (pp. 111–154). American Enterprise Institute Press.
Dabić, M., Vlačić, B., Paul, J., Dana, L. P., Sahasranamam, S., & Glinka, B. (2020). Immigrant entrepreneurship: A review and research agenda. *Journal of Business Research, 113*, 25–38.
Dahlstedt, M., & Hertzberg, F. (red.) (2005). *Demokrati på svenska? Om strukturell diskriminering och politiskt deltagande.* SOU 2005:112. Kulturdepartementet. Utredningen om makt, integration och strukturell diskriminering. Fritzes.
Dahlstedt, M., & Hertzberg, F. (2007). Democracy the Swedish way? The exclusion of 'immigrants' in Swedish politics. *Scandinavian Political Studies, 30*(2), 175–203.
de los Reyes, P., Molina, I., & Mulinari, D. (red.) (2002). *Maktens (o)lika förklädnader: Kön, klass & etnicitet i det postkoloniala Sverige: En festskrift till Wuokko Knocke.* Atlas.
Ekberg, J., & Hammarstedt, M. (1999). Egenföretagande bland invandrare. *Arbetsmarknad & Arbetsliv, 5*(3), 207–217.
Ekelund, J. E., & Larsson, J. P. (2023). *Det nya utanförskapet.* Ekerlids förlag.
Evansluong, Q., & Ramírez-Pasillas, M. (2019). The role of family social capital in immigrants' entrepreneurial opportunity creation processes. *International Journal of Entrepreneurship and Small Business, 36*(1–2), 164–188.
Fairlie, R. W. (2013). Minority and immigrant entrepreneurs: Access to financial capital. In A. F. Constant & K. F. Zimmermann (Eds.), *International handbook on the economics of migration* (pp. 153–173). Edward Elgar.
Fairlie, R. W., & Lofstrom, M. (2013). *Immigration and entrepreneurship.* IZA Discussion Paper No. 7669.
Fischer, P. A., & Straubhaar, T. (1996). *Migration and economic integration in the Nordic Common Market.* Nordic Council of Ministers.
Groglopo, A., Ahmadi, F., & Munobwa, J. S. (2023). Structural racism in Sweden: Framing attitudes towards immigrants through the diversity barometer study (2005–2022). *Social Sciences, 12*(7), 421.
Gruber, M., & Rauhut, D. (2024). *Immigrant entrepreneurship beyond the cities in Austria and Sweden: A policy analysis.* A paper presented at the 63rd European Regional Science Association's Congress, 26–30 August 2024 in Terceira Island, Azores, Portugal.
Gustafsson, B., & Zheng, J. (2006). Earnings of immigrants in Sweden, 1978 to 1999. *International Migration, 44*(2), 79–117.

Hällsten, M., Szulkin, R., & Sarnecki, J. (2013). Crime as a price of inequality? The gap in registered crime between childhood immigrants, children of immigrants and children of native Swedes. *British Journal of Criminology, 53*(3), 456–481.

Johnson, A. (2010). *Garpar, gipskatter och svartskallar. Invandrarna som byggde Sverige*. SNS förlag.

Kamali, M. (2016). Integration beyond multiculturalism: Social cohesion and structural discrimination in Sweden. In P. van Aershot & P. Daenzer (Eds.), *The integration and protection of immigrants* (pp. 71–83). Routledge.

Kazlou, A., & Urban, S. (2023). Swedish migration policy liberalization and the new immigrant entrepreneurs. *International Migration, 61*(2), 87–106.

Khosravi, S. (2012). White masks/Muslim names: Immigrants and name-changing in Sweden. *Race & Class, 53*(3), 65–80.

Kingston, C., & Caballero, G. (2009). Comparing theories of institutional change. *Journal of Institutional Economics, 5*(2), 151–180.

Klinthäll, M., Slavnic, Z., Urban, S., Mitchell, C., & Schölin, T. (2016). *Invandring och företagande*. DELMI kunskapsöversikt 2016:7.

Knocke, W., & Hertzberg, F. (2000). *Mångfaldens barn söker sin plats. En studie om arbetsmarknadschanser för ungdomar med invandrarbakgrund*. Svartvitts förlag i samarbete med Arbetslivsinstitutet.

Kofman, E. (1999). Female 'birds of passage' a decade later: Gender and immigration in the European Union. *International Migration Review, 33*(2), 269–299.

Kondoh, K. (2017). *The economics of international immigration*. Springer.

Laine, J., & Rauhut, D. (2018). When reality does not meet expectations: Refugees in Finland and Sweden. In G. Besier & K. Stokłosa (Eds.), *How to deal with refugees? Europe as a Continent of Dreams* (pp. 61–76). LIT Verlag.

Lundborg, P., & Skedinger, P. (2016). Employer attitudes towards refugee immigrants: Findings from a Swedish survey. *International Labour Review, 155*(2), 315–337.

Lundh, C., & Ohlsson, R. (1994a). *Från arbetskraftsimport till flyktinginvandring*. SNS förlag.

Lundh, C., & Ohlsson, R. (1994b). Immigration and economic change. In T. Bengtsson (Ed.), *Population, economy, and welfare in Sweden* (pp. 87–107). Springer.

Lundh, C., Bennich-Björkman, L., Ohlsson, R., Pedersen, P. J., & Rooth, D. O. (2002). *Arbete? Var god dröj! Invandrare i välfärdssamhället*. SNS förlag.

Macuchova, Z., & Rauhut, D. (2023). Measuring immigrant integration—How, what and for whom? In D. Rauhut (Ed.), *New methods and theory on immigrant integration: Insights from remote and peripheral areas* (pp. 123–141). Edward Elgar.

Magnusson, L. (2001). Invandring och segregation: En bakgrund. In L. Magnussin (red.), *Den delade staden: Segregation och etnicitet i stadsbygden* (pp. 9–24). Boréa bokförlag.

March, J. G., & Olsen, J. P. (1986). Popular sovereignty and the search for appropriate institutions. *Journal of Public Policy, 6*(4), 341–370.

March, J. G., & Olsen, J. P. (1989). *Rediscovering institutions. The organizational basis of politics*. Free Press.
Miao, C. (2020). Immigrant self-employment and local unemployment in Sweden. *The Manchester School, 88*(3), 464–488.
Milgrom, P., North, D., & Weingast, B. (1990). The role of institutions in the revival of trade: The law merchant, private judges and the champagne fairs. *Economics and Politics, 2*(1), 1–23.
Morokvasic, M. (1984). Birds of passage are also women. *International Migration Review, 18*(4), 886–907.
Muhr, A. (2020). *Andra generationens unga företagare med utländsk bakgrund. En förståelse av det egna företagandet utifrån social position*. Linnaeus University Dissertations 374/2020. Linneus University Press.
Muñoz-Mora, J. C., Aparicio, S., Martinez-Moya, D., & Urbano, D. (2022). From immigrants to local entrepreneurs: Understanding the effects of migration on entrepreneurship in a highly informal country. *International Journal of Entrepreneurial Behavior & Research, 28*(9), 78–103.
Neergaard, A. (2002). Fackföreningsrörelsen i ett rasifierat samhälle. In P. de los Reyes, I. Molina, & D. Mulinari (red.), *Maktens (o)lika förklädnader. Kön, klass & etnicitet i det postkoloniala Sverige* (pp. 121–149). Atlas.
Nijkamp, P., Poot, J., & Sahin, M. (Eds.). (2012). *Migration impact assessment*. Edward Elgar.
Nordlund, S. (1999). Invandrarföretagande i Sverige—En historisk tillbakablick. In Kulturdepartementet, *Invandrare som företagare*, SOU 1999:49 (pp. 354–364). Regeringskansliet.
Nordström Skans, O., & Åslund, O. (2009). *Segregationen i storstäderna*. SNS förlag.
North, D. (1991). Institutions. *Journal of Economic Perspectives, 5*(1), 97–112.
North, D. C. (1999). *Institutions, institutional change and economic performance*. Cambridge University Press.
North, D. C., & Thomas, R. P. (1973). *The rise of the Western world: A new economic history*. Cambridge University Press.
Ohlsson, H., Broomé, P., & Bevelander, P. (2012). Self-employment of immigrants and natives in Sweden—A multilevel analysis. *Entrepreneurship and Regional Development, 24*(5–6), 405–423.
Piore, M. J. (1979). *Birds of passage*. Cambridge University Press.
Pripp, O. (2001). *Företagande i minoritet: Om etnicitet, strategier och resurser blandassyrier och syrianer i Södertälje*. Mångkulturellt centrum.
Rath, J., & Kloostermann, R. (2000). Outsiders' business: A critical review of research on immigrant entrepreneurship. *International Migration Review, 34*(3), 657–681.
Rauhut, D. (2014). *I moder Sveas ömma famn. Om Flyktinginvandringen till Sverige 1945–1970*. Carlssons förlag.
Rauhut, D. (2020). Integration and informal institutions. *Society, 57*(2), 211–218.

Rauhut, D., & Laine, J. (2023). Theorising immigrant integration: A critical examination. In D. Rauhut (Ed.), *New methods and theory on immigrant integration: Insights from remote and peripheral areas* (pp. 13–32). Edward Elgar.
Rauhut, D., & Rauhut Kompaniets, O. (2018). The impact of immigrant entrepreneurship regional development in Western Sweden. *Romanian Journal of Regional Science, 12*(1), 18–42.
Rauhut, D., Velasco Echeverría, X., Komornicki, T., Czapiewski, K., et al. (2022). *Policy brief: Russian invasion of Ukraine, analysing the refugees flows and possible implications for Cohesion Policy*. ESPON.
Rauhut, D., Aigner-Walder, B., & Schomaker, R. (2023). *The economics of immigration beyond the cities: Theoretical perspectives and empirical insights*. Palgrave Macmillan.
Rosenberg, N., & Birdzell, L. E., Jr. (1986). *How the West grew rich: The economic transformation of the industrial world*. Basic Books.
Sawyer, L. (2006). Att koppla drömmar till verkligheten: Syokonsulenters syn på etnicitet i övergången från grundskola till gymnasium. In L. Sawyer & M. Kamali (red.), *Utbildningens dilemma. Demokratiska ideal och andrafierande praxis. Integrations- och jämställdhetsdepartementet, Utredningen om makt, integration och strukturell diskriminering*. SOU 2006:40 (pp. 187–249). Fritzes.
Schön, L. (2000). *En modern svensk ekonomisk historia*. SNS förlag.
Searle, J. R. (2005). What is an institution? *Journal of Institutional Economics, 1*(1), 1–22.
Simon, J. (2002). *The economic consequences of immigration*. University of Michigan Press.
Slavnic, Z. (2008). *Forskning om invandrares företagande—En litteraturöversikt*. Rapport 2008:08. Nutek.
Slavnic, Z. (2013). Immigrant small business in Sweden: A critical review of the development of a research field. *Journal of Business Administration Research, 2*(1), 29–42.
Stark, O. (1991). *The migration of labor*. Blackwell.
Svanberg, I., & Tydén, M. (1992). *Tusen år av invandring*. Gidlunds bokförlag.
Sweezy, P. M. (1970). *Teorin för den kapitalistiska utvecklingen*. Rabén & Sjögren.
Tavassoli, S., & Trippl, M. (2019). The impact of ethnic communities on immigrant entrepreneurship: Evidence from Sweden. *Regional Studies, 53*(1), 67–79.
Tempsch, R. (1997). *Från Centraleuropa till Folkhemmet: Den sudet-tyska invandringen till Sverige 1938–1955*. Meddelanden från Ekonomisk-historiska institutionen vid Göteborgs universitet, nr. 73. Akademisk avhandling, Göteborgs universitet.
Tovatt, C. (2016). Det sociala kapitalets betydelse för att få en plats på arbetsmarknaden. In M. Dahlstedt, F. Hertzberg, S. Urban, & A. Ålund (red.), *Utbildning, arbete, medborgarskap: Strategier för inkludering i den mångetniska staden* (pp. 299–320). Boréa Bokförlag.
Zalkat, G. (2024). *Immigrant entrepreneurship in Sweden: Challenges and opportunities related to business development*. PhD Thesis. Halmstad University Press.

CHAPTER 2

Methodological Considerations

Abstract This chapter discusses key definitions and limitations in scope as well as data availability and literature selection. Moreover, the periods in immigrant entrepreneurship are also defined.

Keywords Definitions • Entrepreneurship classification • Legal frameworks • Methodology • Periodisation

2.1 Key Definitions

2.1.1 Migrants and Immigrants

A ‘migrant’ is a person who moves to another country (Castles & Miller, 2009). An ‘immigrant’ refers to a person who is born abroad; the children of immigrants are referred to as ‘second-generation’ immigrants (Dana, 2007). As EU citizens have the same civic rights as natives in other EU countries according to the Maastricht Treaty (European Union, 1992), EU citizens are not considered as immigrants in a legal sense. EU citizens can enter the labour market directly and they are not subject to any integration policies within the EU countries (Mügge & van der Haar, 2016).

D. Rauhut, *Immigrant Entrepreneurship in Sweden*,
https://doi.org/10.1007/978-3-032-02466-4_2

Hence, an immigrant is a non-EU citizen. The term Third Country Nationals (TCN) is used for non-EU citizens.[1]

For this study, the legal difference between 'immigrant' and 'TCN' does not create a bias historically, but it does for the period after 1995 when Sweden became an EU Member State. Before Sweden became an EU Member State, e.g., German, Polish, or Greek citizens starting a company in Sweden were immigrant entrepreneurs. After the Swedish accession to the European Union, the very same entrepreneurs suddenly were considered non-immigrant entrepreneurs.

2.1.2 Immigrant Entrepreneurship

'Entrepreneurship' is generally understood as the undertaking of entrepreneurial activities (Nazareno et al., 2018). To start a limited company in Sweden today, the person needs to be at least 18 years old. However, it is possible to start a trading company or sole proprietorship if a person has turned 16 with the permission of the guardian(s) (Skatteverket, 2024). A citizen of an EU/EEA country has the right to live in an EU country that is not their country of origin, if they can support themselves. Hence, an EU/EEA citizen can start and run a business without a residence permit in Sweden. If the person is a citizen of a country outside the EU/EEA and is to stay in Sweden for longer than three months to run their own business, the person must have a residence permit. The residence permit must be ready before entering Sweden. The Tax Agency assigns the immigrant a coordination number in connection with the company being approved for a VAT-number (Verksamt, 2024). *Coordination number* refers to a unique identification number assigned to certain individuals who are not eligible for a regular Swedish personal identity number but still need to be registered for certain purposes.

For non-EU/EEA citizens, the Migration Agency will make a financial assessment of the applicant's business plans for a residence permit to be granted (Migrationsverket, 2023). The applicant must be able to demonstrate that s/he can make a living now and that there is sufficient capital to

[1] According to the European Commission (n.d.), TCN reside legally in the EU and are the target of EU integration policies. A TCN is 'any person who is not a citizen of the European Union within the meaning of Art. 20(1) of TFEU and who is not a person enjoying the European Union right to free movement, as defined in Art. 2(5) of the Regulation (EU) 2016/399 (Schengen Borders Code)' (European Commission, n.d.).

run the business and support the applicant for at least two years to come. It is possible to add up the income from several jobs and the company (Tillväxtverket, 2017).

Both asylum seekers and 'newly arrived' persons can start a business in Sweden. Asylum seekers can start a business when submitting the asylum application; new arrivals can start a company on the same terms as Swedish citizens. A *newly arrived* is a person who has just received a permanent or temporary residence permit (Verksamt, 2024). Asylum seekers who have started a company cannot change tracks (i.e., visa category) if the asylum application is rejected. However, asylum seekers who have been employed for four months and have a promise of at least 12 months of continued employment can, after a rejection of their asylum application, change tracks and apply for a work permit or start a company (Tillväxtverket, 2017).

During the period 1864 to 1968, immigrant entrepreneurship was ruled by the Business Freedom Ordinance of 1864. This ordinance discriminated immigrant entrepreneurs in several ways. The main characteristics of the regulation are described in the following way:

> In order to obtain permission to operate a business, the foreigner must demonstrate that he/she was of good morals, that the intended business was "avail" for Sweden, did not compete with domestic business and did not contravene Swedish business practice /.../ the foreigner must show security for three years' taxes to the state and municipality. (Nordlund, 1999a, p. 358)

The consequence was that many citizens waited to start a company until they became Swedish citizens (Nordlund, 1999a, p. 358) or started a company in partnership with a Swedish citizen (Najib, 1994). The Business Freedom Ordinance of 1864 was still implemented until the end of 1968, which meant that foreigners who wanted to start a small business were still discriminated against. As an adjustment to the economic integration in Europe—first Sweden's entry into EFTA and then later the European Union—the restrictions concerning the rights of foreigners to start up small business in Sweden were gradually dismantled until 1990 (Nordlund, 1999a, 1999b).

Before the introduction of the Business Freedom Ordinance in 1864, business freedom for foreign entrepreneurs in Sweden was regulated. Foreign entrepreneurs were not equal to domestic entrepreneurs. During the late Middle Ages, for example, the right to conduct retail trade in the cities was restricted, and during the seventeenth and eighteenth centuries, foreigners who wanted to start a business in Sweden had to give up their foreign citizenship. Furthermore, until the middle of the eighteenth century, it was only permitted for foreigners to conduct wholesale trade in the so-called 'staple cities'. Staple cities were a kind of economic free zones where foreign entrepreneurs were attracted with special privileges such as tax breaks, the right to practice religion and legal freedoms. The special 'Jewish regulations' introduced by King Gustav III in 1782 were aimed at attracting wealthy Jews to the big cities of Stockholm, Gothenburg, Norrköping and Karlskrona at the time. To a great extent, the activities of the foreign entrepreneurs in Sweden before 1864 were regulated by various kinds of privileges from the king (Nordlund, 1999a, 1999b).

Today, EU citizens are, as stated in the Maastricht Treaty 1992, not considered immigrants if they reside in another EU country. Consequently, EU citizens starting companies in Sweden since Sweden became an EU Member State in 1995 cannot be classified as immigrant entrepreneurs. Moreover, the group 'immigrants' contains a heterogeneous group of people—to say the least! Asylum seekers have come to Sweden to seek refuge from a troublesome situation in their native country and in case they are granted refugee status, those starting a company in Sweden can be classified as refugee entrepreneurs. Among the non-refugee immigrants, the cause of stay in Sweden is dominated by job offers (labour migrants), studies (students), and family reunion (tied movers). There are also immigrants who have applied for an entrepreneurship visa, i.e., the cause of stay in Sweden is to start a company. As noted earlier in this chapter, asylum seekers who have been denied refugee status may apply for an 'entrepreneurship visa', and hence these asylum seekers will be classified as entrepreneurs.

In this essay, an immigrant entrepreneur is an immigrant, who has resettled in a new country apart from his native country or country of origin and establishes a business venture which creates value. This definition includes both refugees and non-refugees. A refugee entrepreneur is a person who arrives in Sweden as an asylum seeker and starts a company before or after the entrepreneur has obtained a refugee status. When it comes to labour migrants and students who come up with a business idea and, hence, start a company in Sweden are classified as immigrant

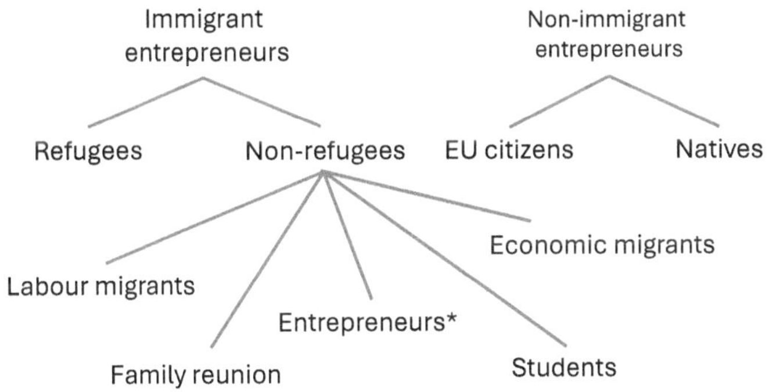

Fig. 2.1 Classification of immigrant entrepreneurship. Own elaboration. * Includes asylum seekers who were not granted refugee status in Sweden and then applied for an entrepreneurship visa

entrepreneurs. This is also valid for the tied movers[2] and economic migrants[3] starting a company in Sweden. The classification of different kinds of immigrant entrepreneurship is illustrated in Fig. 2.1.

2.1.3 Privileged and Disadvantaged Immigrant Entrepreneurs

Privilege and disadvantage have existed in immigrant entrepreneurship throughout history, however materialising differently during different periods. In a simple definition of *privileged immigrant entrepreneurs*, these entrepreneurs enjoy advantages other immigrant entrepreneurs, or even entrepreneurs, do not enjoy (Dheer, 2018). In the Middle Ages some immigrants received a 'Letter of Privilege' by the king, allowing them to run their business under favourable conditions, such as e.g., tax exemption

[2] *Tied movers* refer to individuals or families who relocate due to the employment or career opportunities of another household member, often a spouse or partner. Their decision to move is not primarily driven by their own career aspirations but rather by the need to support or remain with the primary income earner (Freitas-Monteiro, 2024; Banerjee & Phan, 2015).

[3] An *economic migrant* is an individual who moves from one country or region to another primarily for the purpose of improving their economic prospects and living standards. This migration is driven by the pursuit of better employment opportunities, higher wages, improved working conditions, and overall better economic circumstances. Unlike refugees or asylum seekers, economic migrants are not necessarily fleeing from persecution, conflict, or natural disasters; their primary motivation is economic betterment (Ratha et al., 2011; Nathan, 2014).

(Heckscher, 1949; Magnusson, 1999). Today, EU citizens starting a company in another EU country do so under the same set of rules as the natives, while TCNs who start companies in the same EU country operate under another set of regulations (se discussion above).

A simple definition of *disadvantaged immigrant entrepreneurs* is an immigrant entrepreneur not enjoying the same conditions as other (immigrant) entrepreneurs and this disadvantage is set by laws or regulations (Dheer, 2018). Being an immigrant entrepreneur to Sweden during the period for which immigrant entrepreneurship was regulated by the 1864 Business Freedom Ordinance placed the immigrant entrepreneur in a disadvantaged position. Today, non-EU citizens who want to start a company in the EU face disadvantages because of their citizenship status. However, 'disadvantage' could mean more than a legal or institutional framework. Disadvantage also materialises around e.g., social status of what the entrepreneur works with, his/her language proficiency, ability to find employment on the regular labour market, racism and discrimination, and if the immigrant entrepreneur has moved by his/her free choice or is a refugee (Girling, 2022; Ram et al., 2017). This is more about what values, norms, and preferences exist towards immigrant entrepreneurs in the host society.

Considering the existing research gap on *privileged immigrant entrepreneurs* as well as *disadvantaged immigrant entrepreneurs*, future research needs to elaborate more on these concepts. Being privileged or disadvantaged makes a difference for entrepreneurs.

2.2 Limitations in Scope

Until 1809, Finland was an integral part of the Swedish Empire. The cession of Finland resulted in Sweden losing one-third of its land area and one-quarter of its population to Russia. Urban life in Finland was comparable to that in other regions of Sweden, with Turku and Helsinki being the principal cities, characterised by commerce, craftsmanship, and royal administration. These cities also hosted a diverse population, including immigrants and immigrant entrepreneurs (Meinander, 2006). Nevertheless, this essay primarily examines immigrant entrepreneurship within the contemporary borders of Sweden. Including Finland would necessitate the inclusion of Swedish territories in Estonia, Latvia, and northern Germany, which would significantly expand the scope of this study and require extensive research.

Furthermore, the regions that Sweden annexed from Denmark in 1658 (Skåne, Blekinge, Halland, Bohuslän, and Jämtland) are discussed solely when they became part of Sweden. The Hanseatic League established several cities in Scania for trade purposes during the early Middle Ages (Skansjö, 1997). Consequently, the influence of foreign merchants in Scania was significant. Once again, including immigrant business activities prior to 1658 in the regions Sweden acquired from Denmark would be highly resource-intensive, as historical knowledge from this period is as fragmentary in Denmark as it is in Sweden. Generally, the trends and development during the Middle Ages in e.g., Scania during the Danish rule (see e.g., Wetterberg, 2016, 2017; Carelli, 2012; Skansjö, 2012) display similarities to what happened in Sweden.

There is no statistical information in Sweden on self-employment, micro-companies, and small business companies prior to 1990. In the early 1990s, most municipalities in Sweden had little, if any, planning, visions, or cooperation with small business entrepreneurs. For most municipalities at this time, immigration and immigrants were not about entrepreneurship, employment or labour market status, but more on refugee reception, housing issues, and social assistance. When immigrant entrepreneurship suddenly boomed during the 1990s, it took researchers, practitioners, and politicians by surprise (Nordlund, 1999b). In the late 1990s, Sweden was one of the countries in the world whose economy is most depending on its big corporations for employment and GDP growth. Small businesses played a minor role (Bergman et al., 1998). That immigrants could contribute to the Swedish economy by starting small businesses was not thought of prior to the 1990s (Nordlund, 1999b), probably because of the unawareness of immigrant entrepreneurship in Sweden at that time (Nordlund, 1999a).

However, some research on immigrant entrepreneurship was undertaken prior to the 1990s, but immigrant entrepreneurship was usually mentioned as a side-track of entrepreneurship in general. Many scholars in economic history have touched immigrant entrepreneurship briefly in their historical studies on entrepreneurs, entrepreneurship, or economic development in Sweden (Heckscher, 1936, 1949, 1963; Gårdlund, 1942; Nordlund, 1989; Schön, 2000; Magnusson, 2002). Regrettably, our understanding of historical immigrant entrepreneurship before 1990 is limited.

2.3 Literature Selection

This study is a literature review using the findings in previous research as the empirical material for analysis. As it took until the 1980s until immigrant entrepreneurship was 'discovered' by scientists in Sweden, the available material is relatively limited and mainly in monographs in which immigrant entrepreneurship is discussed qualitatively (often as a side-effect of something else). After the turn of the millennium, the literature is much richer and is predominantly based on quantitative studies published in peer-reviewed journals. While the sampling strategy (see Hall, 2020) before the boom of quantitative studies is based on simply identifying the few studies discussing immigrant entrepreneurship, the sampling strategy for period after the millennium turn is based on keywords such as immigrant entrepreneurship in combination with Sweden, urban, rural, sector, industry, labour market, immigrant integration, integration policies, unemployment, and self-employment.

The analysis is conducted by using a structured observation system. In practical terms, it means that the analysed material can only be categorised in one way only. To do so, the coding must be adequate (Robson, 2002). In this study, the material was coded following an iterative, grounded theory approach (Rubin & Babbie, 2010). Hence, the coding focuses on in what sectors and industry immigrant entrepreneurship has taken place, where it has taken place geographically, why it has taken place, and what its economic and social impact have been.

2.4 The Periodisation

Nordlund (1999a, 1999b) divides the historical development of immigrant entrepreneurship in Sweden into three periods. Although a division of qualitative material always involves some type of uncertainty or arbitrariness, Nordlund's periodisation appears reasonable as a starting point. As this essay extends to the present day, and does not stop in the 1990s like Nordlund, a separate period that deals with this period has been added. Sweden was hit by a deep recession during the first half of the 1990s which led to a sharp increase in unemployment for mainly immigrants and young people (Lundh et al., 2002). Simultaneously, refugee immigration to Sweden increased dramatically, which meant that the size of the workforce increased. For individuals without own networks and previous experience of the Swedish labour market, self-employment is usually the only way to work for immigrants (Åslund et al., 2006). Consequently, the context in which immigrant entrepreneurship takes place changed due to what happened in the 1990s and hence the period after should be analysed separately.

References

Åslund, O., Erikson, R., Nordström Skans, O., & Sjögren, A. (2006). *Fritt inträde? Ungdomars och invandrares väg till det första arbetet*. SNS förlag.

Banerjee, R., & Phan, M. B. (2015). Do tied movers get tied down? The occupational displacement of dependent applicant immigrants in Canada. *Journal of International Migration and Integration, 16*(2), 333–353.

Bergman, L., Braunerhjelm, P., Fölster, S., Henreksson, M., & Jakobsson, U. (Eds.). (1998). *Konjunkturrådsrapport 1998: Företagaren i välfärdssamhället*. SNS förlag.

Carelli, P. (2012). *Lunds historia—Staten och omlandet. 1. Medeltiden*. Lunds kommun.

Castles, S., & Miller, M. J. (2009). *The age of migration: International population movements in the modern world*. Palgrave Macmillan.

Dana, L. P. (Ed.). (2007). *Handbook of research on ethnic minority entrepreneurship. A co-evolutionary view on resource management*. Edward Elgar.

Dheer, R. J. S. (2018). Entrepreneurship by immigrants: A review of existing literature and directions for future research. *International Entrepreneurship and Management Journal, 14*(3), 555–614.

European Commission. (n.d.). *Third-country national*. Retrieved January 2, 2023, from https://home-affairs.ec.europa.eu/pages/glossary/third-country-national_en

European Union. (1992). The Treaty of the European Union / Treaty of Maastricht. Signed in Maastricht, the Netherlands, 7 February 1992. *Official Journal of the European Communities* (92/C 191/01).

Freitas-Monteiro, T. (2024). Migration motivation and ethnic identity of migrant couples: Tied versus lead movers. *Review of Economics of the Household, 22*(1), 123–145.

Gårdlund, T. (1942). *Industrialismens samhälle. Den svenska arbetarklassens historia*. Tiden.

Girling, R. (2022). Disadvantaged migrant entrepreneurs? The role of nationality and citizenship in realizing privilege. *New Sociological Perspectives, 2*(2), 30–46.

Hall, R. (2020). *Mixing methods in social research*. Sage.

Heckscher, E. F. (1936). *Sveriges ekonomiska historia* (Vol. I:2). Bonniers.

Heckscher, E. F. (1949). *Sveriges ekonomiska historia* (Vol. II:1). Bonniers.

Heckscher, E. F. (1963). *Svenskt arbete och liv*. Aldus.

Lundh, C., Bennich-Björkman, L., Ohlsson, R., Pedersen, P. J., & Rooth, D. O. (2002). *Arbete? Var god dröj! Invandrare i välfärdssamhället*. SNS förlag.

Magnusson, L. (1999). *Merkantilism. Ett ekonomiskt tänkande formuleras.* SNS förlag.

Magnusson, L. (2002). *Sveriges ekonomiska historia.* Prisma.

Meinander, H. (2006). *Finlands historia. Linjer, strukturer, vändpunkter.* Söderström.

Migrationsverket. (2023). *Uppehållstillstånd för dig som har eget företag.* Retrieved April 12, 2024, from https://www.migrationsverket.se/Privatpersoner/Arbeta-i-Sverige/Eget-foretag.html

Mügge, L., & van der Haar, M. (2016). Who is an immigrant and who requires integration? Categorizing in European Policies. In B. Garcés-Mascareñas & R. Penninx (Eds.), *Integration processes and policies in Europe* (pp. 77–90). Springer.

Najib, A. (1994). *Immigrant small business in Uppsala. Disadvantage in labour market and success in small business activities.* PhD Thesis, Uppsala University, Sweden.

Nathan, M. (2014). The wider economic impacts of high-skilled migrants: A survey of the literature for receiving countries. *IZA Journal of Migration, 3*, 4. https://doi.org/10.1186/2193-9039-3-4

Nazareno, J., Zhou, M., & You, T. (2018). Global dynamics of immigrant entrepreneurship: Changing trends, ethnonational variations, and reconceptualizations. *International Journal of Entrepreneurial Behavior & Research, 25*(5), 780–800.

Nordlund, S. (1989). *Upptäckten av Sverige. Utländska direktinvesteringar i Sverige 1895–1945.* Umeå Studies in Economic History no. 12. Department of Economic History, Umeå University.

Nordlund, S. (1999a). Invandrarföretagande i Sverige—en historisk tillbakablick. In Kulturdepartementet, *Invandrare som företagare*, SOU 1999:49 (pp. 354–364). Regeringskansliet.

Nordlund, S. (1999b). Kommentarer eller synpunkter rörande insatser för att åstadkomma lika behandling av rörelseidkare oavsett etnisk och kulturell bakgrund. In Kulturdepartementet, *Invandrare som företagare*, SOU 1999:49 (pp. 346–353). Regeringskansliet.

Ram, M., Jones, T., & Villares-Varela, M. (2017). Migrant entrepreneurship: Reflections on research and practice. *International Small Business Journal, 35*(1), 3–18.

Ratha, D., Mohapatra, S., & Scheja, E. (2011). *Impact of migration on economic and social development.* The World Bank Policy Research Working Paper 5558. Retrieved January 22, 2025, from https://documents1.worldbank.org/curated/en/617151468332982240/pdf/WPS5558.pdf

Robson, C. (2002). *Real world research.* Blackwell.

Rubin, A., & Babbie, E. (2010). *Research methods for social work.* Brooks/Cole Cengage.

Schön, L. (2000). *En modern svensk ekonomisk historia*. SNS förlag.
Skansjö, S. (1997). *Skånes historia*. Historiska media.
Skansjö, S. (2012). *Lunds historia—Staden och omlandet. 2. Tidigmodern tid*. Lunds kommun.
Skatteverket. (2024). *Starta och registrera företag*. Retrieved April 12, 2024, from https://www.skatteverket.se/foretag/drivaforetag/startaochregistrera.4.58d555751259e4d661680006123.html
Tillväxtverket. (2017). *Starta företag i Sverige*. Retrieved April 12, 2024, from https://tillvaxtverket.se/download/18.6855bfcf184896002ffa1f/1668765691293/Starta%20fo%CC%88retag%20i%20Sverige%20-%20svenska.pdf
Verksamt. (2024). *Starta företag som asylsökande eller nyanländ*. Retrieved April 12, 2024, from https://verksamt.se/starta-foretag/starta-foretag-som-utlandsk-medborgare/starta-foretag-som-asylsokande-eller-nyanland
Wetterberg, G. (2016). *Skånes historia Band 1: 11 500 f.Kr. – 1375 e.Kr*. Albert Bonniers förlag.
Wetterberg, G. (2017). *Skånes historia Band 2: 1376–1720*. Albert Bonniers förlag.

CHAPTER 3

Periods in Immigrant Entrepreneurship

Abstract The aim of this chapter is to describe the immigrant entrepreneurship in Sweden and how it has developed over time. The focus is on the empirical findings and the key questions are: Who are the immigrant entrepreneurs? Where did they come from? Why did they start a company in Sweden? In what sector and industry did they operate?

Keywords Marginalisation vs integration • Sectoral shifts • Ethnic enclaves • Regulatory frameworks • Historical periodisation

3.1 The Period Up to the Mid-Nineteenth Century

For long, Sweden was a poor and undeveloped country in the European periphery. The country was dominated by an agrarian economy, which suffered from chronic shortages of capital, knowledge, technology, and skilled labour. Attracting skilled, capital-strong, and ambitious entrepreneurs from other countries was one way of dealing with these problems (Behre et al., 1985; Berend & Ranki, 1982). In the early Middle Ages, merchants did not only bring capital, knowledge and technology to Sweden, but also Christianity (Bloch, 1993). During the Middle Ages, it was mostly German merchants and craftsmen who came to

D. Rauhut, *Immigrant Entrepreneurship in Sweden*,
https://doi.org/10.1007/978-3-032-02466-4_3

Sweden. Their capital and connections contributed to Sweden being tied closer to the markets of medieval Europe. In this way, they created long-term economic effects on Swedish mining, urban industries, foreign trade, and economic growth (Heckscher, 1936). However, in 1350 due to continuous conflicts with native interests, King Magnus Eriksson tried to reduce the foreign influence in the city magistrates (Nordlund, 1999).

During the late Middle Ages, for example, foreign entrepreneurs were not equal to domestic entrepreneurs. The right to conduct retail trade in the cities was restricted for foreigners, and during the seventeenth and eighteenth centuries, foreigners who wanted to start a business in Sweden had to give up their foreign citizenship. Furthermore, until the middle of the eighteenth century, it was only permitted for foreigners to conduct wholesale trade in the so-called 'staple cities'.[1] Staple cities were a kind of economic free zones where foreign entrepreneurs were attracted with special privileges such as tax breaks, the right to practice religion and legal freedoms. The special 'Jewish regulations' introduced by King Gustav III in 1782 were aimed at attracting wealthy Jews to the big cities of Stockholm, Gothenburg, Norrköping, and Karlskrona at the time (Nordlund, 1999). To a great extent, the activities of the foreign entrepreneurs in Sweden before 1864 were regulated by various kinds of privileges from the king.

Influenced by the mercantilist ideas, during the seventeenth and eighteenth centuries the Swedish state tried to attract knowledgeable foreigners. Through industrial and commercial enterprise, the foreigners would exploit and refine domestic resources and then export them. The aim was to give the country increased income and make the country more self-sufficient. To attract these foreigners, privileges were offered in the form of tax breaks, the right to practice religion and certain legal freedoms. During this time, the immigrants came mainly from Holland, Scotland, England, and the German countries, and they mainly settled in the larger trading cities (Heckscher, 1949; Magnusson, 1999).

[1] Originally, 'staple cities' (stapelstäder) referred to Swedish towns with the right to engage in import and export activities. From the early 1800s, it denoted cities where foreign ships could clear their cargo through customs, essentially cities with port duties (Magnusson, 2002).

3.2 The Period Between the Mid-Nineteenth Century and World War II

The business climate and the conditions for immigrant entrepreneurship transformed during the early nineteenth century. The industrialisation that began in parts of Europe made a country as rich in natural resources as Sweden interesting. Sweden, in turn, became more aware of its comparative advantages in an international liberal economy. The state no longer saw any advantage in encouraging talented foreign entrepreneurs to conduct their business from Sweden. Instead, it became more important to protect domestic interests and control foreign interests. The previous equality between domestic and foreign men was abolished, which resulted in foreigners having to have explicit permission from the Crown to conduct business activities. With the introduction of the Business Freedom Ordinance (Näringsfrihetsförordningen) of 1864, the opportunities for foreigners to conduct business in Sweden changed radically. While the regulation meant an extensive liberalisation of the business world, it was directly discriminatory against immigrant businesses (Gårdlund, 1942). This regulation applied, with some minor changes, until the end of the 1960s (Rauhut, 2014). To obtain authorisation for business operations, a foreign citizen must prove good moral character, ensure Sweden the proposed business benefits, avoid competition with local enterprises, and comply with Swedish business standards. Additionally, the individual must provide security for state and municipal taxes for a period of three years. The consequence was that many citizens waited to start a company until they became Swedish citizens, according to Nordlund (1999). However, it was possible to circumvent this regulation if you started a company together with a Swedish citizen (Najib, 1994).

Moreover, stock market companies, which emerged during the second half of the nineteenth century, offered possibilities for foreigners to be owners of Swedish companies. During the late nineteenth century, it was common for Swedish limited liability companies to write promissory notes with trading houses in Europe to finance their operations. In cases where the promissory note could not be redeemed, the debt was usually converted into shares in the stock company (Jörberg, 1988). When it comes to foreign direct investments 1895–1945, more than half of them were made by Danish and Norwegian investors. German and American direct investments in Sweden were also important. Before World War I, the investments targeted manufacturing companies, which stimulated the consumer goods industry. In the interwar years, most of the foreign direct investments targeted chemical and engineering industries. Sweden also introduced new legislation in 1916 that severely limited foreign investment in the raw materials sector (Nordlund, 1989).

While foreign small business owners were discriminated against by the Business Freedom Ordinance, international capital could circumvent the same regulation. Especially foreign family business owners were treated with suspicion and were disliked during the end of the nineteenth century up to the 1940s. As the Swedish industrial capacity winded up, skilled labour was needed. Foreign skilled workers were welcome to work, but not others. During the period from mid-nineteenth century until World War I, many refugees, mostly Jews from today's Ukraine, Russia, Lithuania and Poland, arrived in Sweden seeking refuge. However, the Business Freedom Ordinance of 1864 prevented them from becoming entrepreneurs in Sweden. The attitude towards Jewish entrepreneurship remained very negative during the interwar years and after 1933 attempts were made by small business owners' associations in Sweden to keep the small business owner sector 'Aryan'. Most foreigners obtaining a permit to set up their business in Sweden came from Norway and Germany during the period from mid-nineteenth century until World War II and they mainly engaged in activities in the manufacturing, trade, and craft sectors. Germans, Scots, English, and Danes started businesses in industries such as brewing, trade, machine workshops, and in the textile and forestry industries (Nordlund, 1999). For the period 1880–1910, immigrant entrepreneurs were 1.2 percent more likely to be factory owners compared to native entrepreneurs. Immigrants from Denmark, Norway, Poland, and the UK were the most entrepreneurial in Sweden during this period (Jensen, 2021).[2]

3.3 The Period Between World War II and the Mid-1990s

After World War II, Sweden became a country of immigration. The Swedish industrial sector cried for labour, which was imported from mainly Finland, Turkey, Yugoslavia, and Greece. Smaller groups of labour

[2] Notably, Norway and Sweden had the same king, and were hence in a political union, until Norway declared independence in 1905. Moreover, Poland did not exist as an independent country during the period Jensen (2021) analyses; the country was split between German, Russian, and the Habsburg empires.

migrants came from Hungary and Italy (Svanberg & Tydén, 1992). Displaced persons as well as labour immigrated to Sweden from Germany (Rauhut, 2014; Tempsch, 1997). What Sweden demanded was workers, not entrepreneurs (Lundh & Ohlsson, 1994; Rauhut, 2019). Generally, refugees were sent to work as unskilled labour in the industrial sector, regardless their educational background (Byström, 2012).

The Business Freedom Ordinance of 1864 was still implemented until the end of 1968, which meant that foreigners who wanted to start a small business were still discriminated against. As an adjustment to the economic integration in Europe—first Sweden's entry into EFTA and then later the European Union—the restrictions concerning the rights of foreigners to start up small business in Sweden were gradually dismantled until 1990 (Nordlund, 1999). Parallel to this development, Sweden entered a structural economic crisis in the 1970s, which brought the demand for foreign labour to the industrial sector to an abrupt end. Moreover, the refugee flows from Western Asia, Latin America, and Africa started to increase during the 1970s (Lundh & Ohlsson, 1994).

Between 1960 and 1990, the share of immigrant small business ownership increased from generally ca 3 percent to ca 10 percent. Most immigrant companies started in the bigger cities; in the big cities Eskilstuna and Västerås and the metropolitan Gothenburg, the share of immigrant small business ownership increased from generally ca 5 percent to ca 15 percent during the same period. Only a few of the immigrants owning a small business were non-Europeans up to the 1980s; in 1990 every fourth small business was run by a non-European immigrant. The most entrepreneurial immigrants were men, and they came from Denmark and Germany. Among the refugees, Polish, Hungarian, and the Baltic countries were most entrepreneurial. Among women, Polish women were most entrepreneurial. These immigrants were successful in the hotel and restaurant sectors. However, many immigrant entrepreneurs were also successful in the construction and engineering industry as well as in the retail trade sector and service sector in general (Nordlund, 1999). The incomes levels of the immigrant small business owners were significantly lower than for those of Swedish small business owners, which indicates that immigrant entrepreneurs operated in sectors with low profitability (Gustafsson et al., 1990).

The list of successful immigrant entrepreneurs during the 1950s, 1960s, and 1970s is quite substantial. Many well-known 'Swedish' companies were started up by immigrants during this period (Johnson, 2010). However, we need to keep in mind, that many of these companies were founded in partnership with a Swedish citizen (Najib, 1994), or that the immigrants waited to start the company until they became Swedish citizens (Nordlund, 1999). The expansion of immigrant entrepreneurs since the 1970s correlates with the increasing difficulties for immigrants to enter the regular labour market and can, hence, be seen as a survival strategy for a marginal position at the labour market (Gür & Hellman, 1996).

3.4 The Period After the Mid-1990s

During the 1990s, it became clear that the refugee immigrants of the 1970s and 1980s had problems to establish themselves in the Swedish labour market (Lundh & Ohlsson, 1994). The conclusion about the immigrant entrepreneurship of the 1990s is bleak. The marginalisation of these immigrants is 'moved from the exclusion of unemployment and made invisible in the form of the economic marginalisation of business' (NUTEK, 2001, p. 91). Much of the immigrant entrepreneurship has come to be concentrated in low-productive and labour-intensive industries with a small profit margin. For example, restaurants, taxis, hairdressers, convenience stores, retail, cleaning companies, and personal services are industries that dominate immigrant entrepreneurship. Many of these areas are also cyclically sensitive (Rauhut & Rauhut Kompaniets, 2018).

Sweden was one of the European countries that received the most refugees in relation to its population during the 2010s. An overwhelming majority of these were refugees and low-educated people from Africa and Asia. No integration into the Swedish labour market has taken place, let alone integrated into Swedish society (Ekelund & Larsson, 2023). In many cases, these immigrants have formed clusters in the suburbs of large cities and thus formed ethnic enclaves (Edin et al., 2003; Hårsman, 2006). In these ethnic enclaves, some have become entrepreneurs, offering goods and services to their compatriots (Andersson & Hammarstedt, 2015; Andersson & Larsson, 2016; Hammarstedt, 2006). Furthermore, in these ethnic enclaves there are networks among compatriots who can help with financing (Aldén & Hammarstedt, 2016), and to other immigrant entrepreneurs within their own group who can help (Tavassoli & Trippl, 2019; Andersson et al., 2021). The conclusion is that labour with no matching demand needs to find a source of living, and entrepreneurship represents such alternative. Most immigrants who become entrepreneurs produce goods and services for their compatriots in ethnical enclaves. To what extent this enhances their inclusion in the Swedish society can be questioned.

3.5 Summary and Conclusion

Sweden's history reflects a complex interplay between foreign entrepreneurs, labour migration, and economic policies, shaping the country's economic landscape and social dynamics over time. The role of immigrant entrepreneurs continues to evolve, impacting both economic growth and social integration. In Table 3.1, the main characteristics of the four periods are summarised schematically.

The role of immigrant entrepreneurs has been a consistent feature in Sweden's economic landscape. From German merchants and craftsmen in the Middle Ages to immigrant entrepreneurs from e.g., Denmark, Germany, the Netherlands and Scotland, and later, after World War II refugees from Poland, Hungary, and the Baltic countries to the more recent refugees from outside Europe, immigrants have always been involved in shaping Sweden's business environment. Moreover, throughout the history described, Sweden's economy has been shaped by immigration. Starting from the Middle Ages, Sweden consistently sought to integrate immigrants into its economy—initially focusing on attracting ambitious foreign entrepreneurs and later, after the industrialisation in the late nineteenth century, on immigrant labour to meet industrial demands. After World War II, the labour immigration was organised by the State. The dependence on immigration marks a continuity throughout history.

However, there are also several aspects of change throughout history. (1) The primary focus of immigration policies shifted significantly over time. Initially, there was an effort to attract foreign entrepreneurs to stimulate economic development. However, during the early nineteenth century, this focus changed to support domestic entrepreneurs, evident with the enactment of the Business Freedom Ordinance of 1864, which transformed business opportunities but also discriminated against immigrant businesses. (2) Post-World War II, the trend shifted from emigration to immigration, with Sweden attracting labour to fulfil industrial needs, particularly for unskilled labourers. This period also saw changes in policies that gradually dismantled restrictions, allowing for increased immigrant small business ownership. (3) In the 1990s, a new challenge emerged with refugees, particularly from Asia and Africa, facing difficulties in integrating into the labour market. This led to the formation of ethnic enclaves and a concentration of immigrant entrepreneurship in labour-intensive, low-productive sectors, a significant departure from the earlier periods when immigrant businesses flourished in diverse and often higher-productive sectors.

Table 3.1 A schematic overview of immigrant entrepreneurship during the four periods

	Characteristics	*Policy aim*	*Policies*	*Migration*	*Key developments*
Pre-1860s	Underdevelopment and poverty; agrarian economy	Attract foreign entrepreneurs, increase investments in Sweden, increase exports	Royal 'letters of privilege', granting the invited foreigner e.g. tax exemption or religious freedom, monopoly markets	Immigration of invited foreigners to Sweden from economically important countries	Foreign merchants and craftsmen made valuable contributions as immigrant entrepreneurs in Sweden
1860s—World War II	Industrialisation begins; liberal economic focus	Stimulate capital accumulation; attract labour; mechanisation of agricultural sector; increase exports; Protect Swedish interests and control foreign interests	Significant institutional change, e.g. through the abolishment of guilds in 1846; first limited liability company law in 1848; Business Freedom Ordinance of 1864. In 1916, a law which significantly reduced foreign investments in the raw material sector was implemented	Emigration of labour, mainly to North America	Capital accumulation increased as did foreign investments and ownership. Sole proprietorship and partnerships were disadvantaged which disfavoured immigrant entrepreneurship in small family businesses; Jews were discriminated

	Characteristics	*Policy aim*	*Policies*	*Migration*	*Key developments*
World War II—1990s	Increasing international competition; The 'golden era' of industrialism 1948–1973; deindustrialisation and the rise of the service economy 1975–1995	Attract foreign labour; economies of scale, increase Swedish exports	Labour immigration was promoted up to 1967; after 1975 the labour immigration is marginal. When labour immigration was prioritised, immigrant entrepreneurship was disfavoured by the fact that it was difficult to start a business if you were not a Swedish citizen	Labour immigration 1948–1967; the extra-European refugee immigration starts in the late 1960s and is dominant in the 1990s	The discrimination of Jewish entrepreneurship stopped after WWII; Sole proprietorship and partnerships were disadvantaged which disfavoured immigrant entrepreneurship. Due to unemployment immigrant entrepreneurship increased from the 1970s and onwards
Post-1990s	The golden era of the service economy up to the Covid-19 pandemic; globalisation	Attract foreign investments, foreign human capital and entrepreneurs; increase exports	Significant institutional change when Sweden became an EU Member State 1995. EU citizens have the same rights as natives and hence are not immigrants; non-EU citizens can apply for an 'entrepreneurship visa'	The extra-European refugee immigration to Sweden dominates; marginal immigration from EU countries	Most immigrant entrepreneurs are refugees in labour-intensive and low-productive sectors; most 'entrepreneurship' visas have been granted to people from Middle East and Africa; ethnic enclaves

Source: Own elaboration

While Sweden's engagement with immigrant entrepreneurs and labour has remained a constant thread, the nature of this engagement and the policies surrounding it have evolved, reflecting changes in economic strategies, labour demands, and immigration patterns. The transformation from attracting skilled foreign entrepreneurs to focusing on domestic entrepreneurship and later addressing the challenges of integrating refugees into the labour market, showcases the dynamic and adaptive nature of Sweden's economic and social policies over time.

References

Aldén, L., & Hammarstedt, M. (2016). Discrimination in the credit market? Access to financial capital among self-employed immigrants. *Kyklos, 69*(1), 3–31.

Andersson, L., & Hammarstedt, M. (2015). Ethnic enclaves, networks and self-employment among Middle Eastern immigrants in Sweden. *International Migration, 53*(6), 27–40.

Andersson, M., & Larsson, J. P. (2016). Local entrepreneurship clusters in cities. *Journal of Economic Geography, 16*(1), 39–66.

Andersson, M., Larsson, J. P., & Öner, Ö. (2021). Ethnic enclaves and self-employment among Middle Eastern immigrants in Sweden: Ethnic capital or enclave size? *Regional Studies, 55*(4), 590–604.

Behre, G., Larsson, L. O., & Österberg, E. (1985). *Sveriges historia 1521–1809*. Esselte Studium.

Berend, I. T., & Ranki, G. (1982). *The European periphery and industrialization 1780–1914*. Akadémiai Kiadó.

Bloch, M. (1993). *Feudal society, Vol. 1: The growth of ties of dependence*. Routledge.

Byström, M. (2012). *Utmaningen. Den svenska välfärdsstatens möte med flyktingar i andra världskrigets tid*. Nordic Academic Press.

Edin, P. A., Fredriksson, P., & Åslund, O. (2003). Ethnic enclaves and the economic success of immigrants—Evidence from a natural experiment. *Quarterly Journal of Economics, 118*(1), 329–357.

Ekelund, J. E., & Larsson, J. P. (2023). *Det nya utanförskapet*. Ekerlids förlag.

Gårdlund, T. (1942). *Industrialismens samhälle. Den svenska arbetarklassens historia*. Tiden.

Gür, T., & Hellman. (1996). *En stjälpande hand—Om invandrarföretagares villkor i Sverige*. Ekonomifakta.

Gustafsson, B., Zamanian-B, M., & Aguilar, R. (1990). *Invandring och försörjning*. Daidalos.

Hammarstedt, M. (2006). The predicted earnings differential and immigrant self-employment in Sweden. *Applied Economics, 38*(6), 619–630.

Hårsman, B. (2006). Ethnic diversity and spatial segregation in the Stockholm region. *Urban Studies, 43*(8), 1341–1364.
Heckscher, E. F. (1936). *Sveriges ekonomiska historia* (Vol. I:2). Bonniers.
Heckscher, E. F. (1949). *Sveriges ekonomiska historia* (Vol. II:1). Bonniers.
Jensen, I. O. R. (2021). *"The Swedish dream"—Immigrant entrepreneurship in Sweden between 1880 and 1910.* Master's Thesis in Economic History, Lund University, Sweden.
Johnson, A. (2010). *Garpar, gipskatter och svartskallar. Invandrarna som byggde Sverige.* SNS förlag.
Jörberg, L. (1988). *Svenska företagare under industrialismens genombrott 1870–1885.* Lund University Press.
Lundh, C., & Ohlsson, R. (1994). *Från arbetskraftsimport till flyktinginvandring.* SNS förlag.
Magnusson, L. (1999). *Merkantilism. Ett ekonomiskt tänkande formuleras.* SNS förlag.
Magnusson, L. (2002). *Sveriges ekonomiska historia.* Prisma.
Najib, A. (1994). *Immigrant small business in Uppsala. Disadvantage in labour market and success in small business activities.* PhD Thesis, Uppsala University, Sweden.
Nordlund, S. (1989). *Upptäckten av Sverige. Utländska direktinvesteringar i Sverige 1895–1945.* Umeå Studies in Economic History no. 12. Department of Economic History, Umeå University.
Nordlund, S. (1999). Invandrarföretagande i Sverige—En historisk tillbakablick. In Kulturdepartementet, *Invandrare som företagare*, SOU 1999:49 (pp. 354–364). Regeringskansliet.
NUTEK. (2001). *Marginalisering eller integration—Invandrares företagande i svensk retorik och praktik.* Nutek.
Rauhut, D. (2014). *I moder Sveas ömma famn.* Carlsons bokförlag.
Rauhut, D. (2019). Arbetskraftsinvandringens drivkrafter 1945–1960—En problematisering och kritik. In D. Rauhut & L. Broström (red.), *Med öppna armar? Om integration och invandring till Sverige 1945–1970* (pp. 205–229). Daidalos.
Rauhut, D., & Rauhut Kompaniets, O. (2018). The impact of immigrant entrepreneurship regional development in Western Sweden. *Romanian Journal of Regional Science, 12*(1), 18–42.
Svanberg, I., & Tydén, M. (1992). *Tusen år av invandring.* Gidlunds bokförlag.
Tavassoli, S., & Trippl, M. (2019). The impact of ethnic communities on immigrant entrepreneurship: Evidence from Sweden. *Regional Studies, 53*(1), 67–79.
Tempsch, R. (1997). *Från Centraleuropa till Folkhemmet: Den sudet-tyska invandringen till Sverige 1938–1955.* Meddelanden från Ekonomisk-historiska institutionen vid Göteborgs universitet, nr. 73. Akademisk avhandling, Göteborgs universitet.

CHAPTER 4

Outcomes and Consequences

Abstract This chapter discusses what the immigrant entrepreneurship resulted in. Four different aspects will be in focus: the spatial patterns of immigrant entrepreneurship, economic consequences, social consequences and what institutional changes immigrant entrepreneurship has led to.

Keywords Spatial patterns • Economic impact • Social integration • Institutional change • Historical continuity and transformation

This chapter discusses the multifaceted outcomes of immigrant entrepreneurship throughout history. By examining four distinct aspects, it aims to provide a comprehensive understanding of its impact. First, the spatial patterns of immigrant entrepreneurship are explored. Second, the economic consequences are analysed, considering both the contributions to local economies and the broader economic implications. Third, the social consequences are discussed, focusing on how immigrant entrepreneurship affects social integration, community dynamics, and intercultural interactions. Finally, the chapter investigates the institutional changes prompted by immigrant entrepreneurship, examining shifts in policies, regulations, and the overall business environment.

D. Rauhut, *Immigrant Entrepreneurship in Sweden*,
https://doi.org/10.1007/978-3-032-02466-4_4

4.1 Geographical Distribution of Immigrant Entrepreneurship

During the Middle Ages, foreign entrepreneurs came to operate mainly from the Swedish cities (Heckscher, 1936). The most important trading cities at this time were Stockholm, Visby, Kalmar, Arboga, and Söderköping (Lindkvist & Ågren, 1985; Arnstberg & Ehn, 1976). In many cities, the foreigners, mainly Germans, came to constitute such a large proportion of the population that the royal power had to limit their political influence (Nordlund, 1999a). This is illustrated in Fig. 4.1.

Even during the mercantilist era, the foreign entrepreneurs mainly settled in the larger Swedish trading cities such as Stockholm, Gothenburg, Norrköping, Karlskrona, and Eskilstuna (Heckscher, 1949). To little surprise, these cities are all coastal cities with ports (see Fig. 4.2).

During the breakthrough of industrialisation at the end of the nineteenth century, it was mainly Gothenburg that attracted foreign entrepreneurs, but also Stockholm (Magnusson, 2002). At the end of the nineteenth century up to and including World War II, it seems that it was mainly refugees among the immigrants who started businesses in Sweden. As they usually had difficulty meeting the requirements stipulated in the Business Freedom Ordinance of 1864, the companies were started after they became Swedish citizens (Nordlund, 1999a). These entrepreneurs often settled in larger cities such as Stockholm, Göteborg, Borås, Landskrona, Motala, Malmö, Örebro, and Sundsvall (see Fig. 4.3). Göteborg was the major immigration city in Sweden until World War II (Svanberg & Tydén, 1992). This distribution of immigrants appears to follow the regional specialisation in the manufacturing sector (Bäcklund, 1996), so it is not surprising to find more immigrant entrepreneurs where immigrants generally settle down.

After World War II, immigration has been dominated by labour and refugees. These two groups have come to be concentrated in the three metropolitan counties and regions with larger industrial cities. As a result of the transition from an industrial economy to an economy dominated by service production, the concentration in large cities has decreased over time. During periods, refugees have also been allocated to sparsely populated regions (Johansson & Rauhut, 2008). Certain refugee nationalities were also prohibited from settling in Stockholm, Göteborg, and Malmö until the 1960s (Rauhut, 2014). When the immigrants then became Swedish citizens, some of them started businesses, with the result that immigrant entrepreneurship largely followed the composition of the population (see Fig. 4.4). The propensity of Middle Eastern immigrants to

Fig. 4.1 Cities in Sweden anno 1350 with the highest share of immigrant entrepreneurs. Source: Own elaboration

Fig. 4.2 Cities in Sweden anno 1700 with the highest share of immigrant entrepreneurs. Source: Own elaboration

Fig. 4.3 Cities in Sweden anno 1890 with the highest share of immigrant entrepreneurs. Source: Own elaboration

Fig. 4.4 Cities in Sweden anno 1970 with the highest share of immigrant entrepreneurs. Source: Own elaboration

Sweden living in ethnic enclaves tends to transcend from having no employment to self-employment if many fellow countrymen in the enclave are business owners, while weak effects emanating from business owners in other groups can be observed. Immigrants appear to be significantly less stimulated by people who do not belong to their own ethnic group (Andersson et al., 2021). The likelihood to have many fellow countrymen around is higher in metropolitan areas than in peripheral and remote areas. A negative correlation can be observed between the share of non-EU citizens outside metropolitan areas and the number of company startups at a regional level in Europe (Rauhut et al., 2022). There is no critical mass within the own ethnical group to start a company, and immigrants not belonging to the same ethnical group do not make up for this, following the argument of Andersson et al. (2021). Hence, most contemporary immigrant entrepreneurship in Sweden takes place in the bigger cities.

4.2 Economic Consequences

It is difficult to assess the economic impact of immigrant entrepreneurship historically. The direct impact, e.g. in terms of stimulating economic growth, is unknown simply because there statistical data does not exist or is too fragmented. What we do know, however, is that throughout history, immigrant entrepreneurship has brought new ideas, products, and services to Sweden. For some of these, the success has come relatively quickly after they have been introduced to the Swedish market, but in other cases the success has been relatively limited. Nordlund (1999a) concludes that immigrant entrepreneurship played a relatively bigger role for the Swedish economy historically than during the twentieth century. From the Middle-Ages throughout the eighteenth century, importing foreign entrepreneurs was not only about importing skilful persons with key competence to develop a certain industry, craft, or trade, but also to attract foreign capital to Sweden as well as to open new destinations for Swedish export. The Hanseatic influence in the Swedish trading cities during the Middle-Ages was massive, and from the trading cities the Hansa controlled the hinterland economically (Heckscher, 1963). The Swedish attitude towards foreign entrepreneurs was generally positive during the Great Power era (1611–1718). The purpose of letting foreigners run companies in Sweden was that the Swedish side wanted to benefit from their capital, education and skills in sectors and industries that Sweden regarded as strategically important to maintain its position of power in Northern Europe (Behre et al., 1985). Such strategic sectors and industries were closely related to war-related production, and means to finance such production (Heckscher, 1963).

It is crucial to acknowledge that the imported entrepreneurs were granted monopolistic concessions when operating in Sweden. In practical terms, this conferred upon them the ability to set prices autonomously, thereby ensuring profitability. Sweden was in dire need of their expertise in trade and business, international networks, and economic resources. Consequently, this facilitated profiteering; these entrepreneurs did not establish businesses in Sweden out of altruism, but rather to amass personal wealth (Arnstberg & Ehn, 1976).

After Sweden lost its status as a regional power in the early eighteenth century, an era of trade policy protectionism began (Magnusson, 1999). The preservation of the Swedish struck hard against anything foreign, including former immigrant entrepreneurs. The economic policy was guided by mercantilist ideals, which meant that Sweden's exports should be as strong as possible while imports should be limited to a minimum. Somewhat paradoxically, skilled foreign labour was both necessary and welcome to achieve this (Svanberg & Tydén, 1992).

Imported entrepreneurs, possessing extensive knowledge of foreign markets, played a pivotal role in the implementation of mercantilist principles in Sweden. The monopolistic concessions granted to these entrepreneurs enabled their merchant houses to amass both wealth and political influence. It is noteworthy that Jewish merchants were prohibited from purchasing land in Sweden; this restriction was based on the belief that land ownership would render them independent of the Crown. The prevailing notion was that all merchants should remain reliant on the goodwill of the Swedish state, thereby ensuring their loyalty (Arnstberg & Ehn, 1976).

It is in this context that the introduction of the 1864 Business Freedom Ordinance should be seen (Nordlund, 1999a). Without the foreign risk capital, either in the form of foreign direct investment or in the form of credits and part ownership, which was added to investments and product development in Sweden, economic development would have been modest (Nordlund, 1989; Jörberg, 1988; Heckscher, 1963). However, the economic importance of immigrant or foreign entrepreneurs in Sweden up to World War II was marginal (Nordlund, 1999a).

After World War II, Sweden still wanted labour migrants, not entrepreneurs. At the same time, immigrants who tried to start small businesses were discriminated against by the state. The Business Freedom Ordinance of 1864 was enforced until the end of 1968 and then a transition period, in which the last obstacles against immigrant entrepreneurship were removed, lasted until 1990 (Nordlund, 1999a). The long-term effects of post-World War II immigration to Sweden displays marginal positive effects on GDP (Ekberg, 1977), while the short-term effects (transfers from immigrants to natives) are positive and account for ca 1 percent of the GDP (Ekberg, 1999; Gustafsson & Österberg, 2001). However, Lundh and Ohlsson (1994b, p. 104) conclude that in the 1960s, the rich supply of low-skilled foreign labour to Sweden 'was inimical to structural economic change. Instead of committing investment to technological measures which would increase productivity (and therefore wages), stagnating firms and branches opted to take on foreign workers'. Instead of expanding intensively, i.e., replacing labour with capital, the industrial expansion in Sweden at this time was extensive, i.e., expanding by using more labour with the same technology (Rauhut, 2019a).

Since the 1990s, immigrant's entrepreneurship in Sweden has mainly dealt with how to put unemployed immigrants into work. If the demand for immigrant (refugee) labour is too low to offer them any employment at the regular labour market, self-employment has been seen as an alternative for them to enter the labour market (Andersson Joona, 2016; Evansluong et al., 2019). As most of these immigrant entrepreneurs come to work in low-productive and labour-intensive sectors and industries, the economic effects are modest if positive at all (Rauhut & Rauhut Kompaniets, 2018).

4.3 Social Consequences

The social consequences of immigrant entrepreneurship can be viewed from several perspectives. How well these immigrant entrepreneurs assimilated or integrated into the Swedish society is one way to approach the question on what social consequences this kind of immigration resulted in. However, it was possible to become an immigrant entrepreneur in different ways. To be invited to come to Sweden to set up your business was one way to become an immigrant entrepreneur at this time, but also to come to Sweden as labour or refugee and then start a business in Sweden after some years. In the latter case, becoming an immigrant entrepreneur reflects a process in which some immigrants become entrepreneurs while others not.

How and to what extent foreign entrepreneurs who moved to Sweden came to be integrated or assimilated during the Middle Ages, we do not know much about. However, it is documented that there were conflicts between these immigrant entrepreneurs and the native ones. The German merchants and craftsmen who moved their business to Sweden tried to strengthen the power of the Hanseatic League in the Swedish cities, something that caused King Magnus Eriksson to limit the power of these immigrants through legislation in 1350. To conduct business in Sweden, one had to give up one's foreign citizenship (Nordlund, 1999a). Sweden was a multi-ethnic country until the beginning of the nineteenth century. In addition to Swedes, e.g., Germans, Danes, Estonians, Karelians, and Finns were a natural part of the Swedish population (Svanberg & Tydén, 1992). The elements of English, Scots, Walloons, and Dutch were also large since many immigrated from these countries during the seventeenth and eighteenth centuries, both as labour and as well as entrepreneurs (Heckscher, 1963). The fact that these immigrants, who were initially Christian and who during the latter part of the seventeenth century and during the eighteenth century were mostly Protestant, means that one can assume that there was a common basis of values with the native population, and this should have facilitated an integration and assimilation. That intermarriage was common between these immigrants and Swedes during this period is documented (Svanberg & Tydén, 1992). Although intermarriages occurred, it is most likely that they happened within the same social strata. We must remember that many of the imported entrepreneurs at this time were part affiliated with affluent merchant houses, possessing substantial economic resources and wielding significant political influence. Consequently, they did not intermingle with the common populace. Furthermore, this immigrant upper class shared minimal commonalities with the foreign craftsmen who independently sought to migrate to Sweden (Arnstberg & Ehn, 1976). Not much has been written about the extent to which labour immigrants and refugees become entrepreneurs after a few years in Sweden before the nineteenth century.

The nature of immigration to Sweden changed in the middle of the nineteenth century. Refugees from Russia—and more specifically the areas that today comprise Poland, Lithuania, and Ukraine—began to come to Sweden. It was predominantly Jews who fled the pogroms that took place in these Russian areas (Nordlund, 1999a). Although Jews had previously been invited to Sweden as entrepreneurs, and then welcomed, times had changed. Due to the Business Freedom Ordinance of 1864, they could not start businesses, and they had difficulty getting jobs. In most cases, becoming one's own business was the only way to support oneself. Many of these Jewish refugees became their own entrepreneurs as soon as they became Swedish citizens (Svanberg & Tydén, 1992). However, the businesses these Jews started—small family businesses, craft and sole proprietorships—were regarded with both suspicion and xenophobia. During the twentieth century until World War II, this became reinforced (Hammar, 1964). In the 1930s and during World War II, the Swedish authorities systematically rejected applications from Jews to run businesses in Sweden, and this did not only apply to Jewish refugees but to Jews in general (Nordlund, 1999a).

While labour immigrants and refugees from the Nordic countries were regarded as *brothers* after World War II, corresponding immigrants from Germany came to be treated as *guests* during the same period. Refugees from e.g., the Baltic countries, Poland, Russia, and Jews were regarded as *parasites* and treated accordingly (Byström, 2006). Many of these immigrant groups came to live a secluded life in Sweden, parallel to the rest of the population (Rauhut, 2014). The integration of refugees in Sweden was not good during this period, but since the refugees were relatively few, the increasing segregation was not considered a problem (Rauhut, 2019b). During the period 1957–1981, the dependence of social assistance among immigrants in Sweden increased sharply, and it was mainly immigrant men who were affected. Previously, these had worked in heavy industry, but these jobs were now rationalised away in Sweden due to increased international competition (Broström & Rauhut, 2018). The labour market situation forced many immigrants to become small business owners to make a living (NUTEK, 2001). Labour immigration to Sweden largely stopped completely at the end of the 1960s. The refugees arriving in Sweden in the 1970s and 1980s often found themselves stuck in unemployment and far from being integrated (Lund & Ohlsson, 1992). Entrepreneurship was one of the few options for making a living for many immigrants (Gür & Hellman, 1996). The development of increasing marginalisation of immigrant entrepreneurs that could be observed during the 1990s, where the marginalisation of immigrants 'moved from the exclusion of unemployment and made invisible in the form of the economic marginalisation of business' (NUTEK, 2001, p. 91), has continued until today. In many cases, public efforts to reduce unemployment in immigrant-dense and segregated residential areas have involved getting the unemployed to become their own entrepreneurs (Ohlsson et al., 2012). Among other things, it is this policy that has created the ethnic enclaves and parallel societies that now exist in Swedish cities (Eklund & Larsson, 2023). For many immigrant entrepreneurs, self-employment is associated with a loss of social status. For people from an upper-middle-class background, self-employment in many cases, and especially if the decision to start one's own business is based on unemployment and exclusion, means failure. Even if you can make a living from your business, many of them feel disappointed (NUTEK, 2001).

Up to and including the end of the 1960s, immigration to Sweden was dominated by European labour immigrants. The proportion of refugees was smaller, and these came from Europe (Rauhut, 2014). Since the 1970s, the composition of immigrants has changed significantly. Labour immigration stopped abruptly in the early 1970s and immigration came to be dominated by refugees from countries outside Europe (Bevelander et al., 1997; Lundh & Ohlsson, 1994a). Already in the 1990s, research showed that these immigrants lacked what was called 'culture-specific capital'. By this is meant, in a broad sense, knowledge of social codes, culture and linguistic competence (Broomé et al., 1998). An understanding among immigrants of this kind of informal institutions is important to be able to become part of the society the person lives in (Rauhut, 2020). Holding on to the informal institutions one had in one's home country and not trying to learn those in the new country makes integration difficult (Rauhut & Laine, 2023). What characterises much of the non-European refugee immigration since the 1970s is that the norms, values and preferences regarding, for example, society, social relations and the labour market—what constitutes informal institutions—are fundamentally different compared to the informal institutions that exist in Sweden, and then the integration of these immigrants becomes difficult (Broomé et al., 1998). The integration of today's refugees from e.g., the Middle East and Africa shows similarities with the challenges the Eastern European Jews who came to Sweden in the second half of the nineteenth century struggled with. In a sense, the obstacles to immigrant entrepreneurship identified today (Carlson & Hikam, 2016; Carlson & Schölin, 2016) imply that these obstacles have been institutionalised.

4.4 Institutional Changes

The policy response on immigrant entrepreneurship has followed the ambitions the king and, later, the parliament and government had regarding Sweden's political and economic development. Consequently, the direction and content of the policies on immigrant entrepreneurship has changed many a time. The same can be said to apply to the regulations that have governed immigrant entrepreneurship in Sweden over time. However, it must be remembered that a change in laws and regulations, i.e. formal institutions, occurs slowly and often in response to changing power relations. A changed legislation aims to ensure the current order or to create a new one.

The institutional framework regulating immigrant entrepreneurship during the pre-industrial area allowed immigrants to become entrepreneurs in Sweden if Sweden benefitted from it. While capital, networks and knowledge that Sweden could benefit from opened for these entrepreneurs, a political influence that did not favour Sweden or that challenged the established power structures inhibited immigrant entrepreneurship.

The Swedish state took on a large and active role during industrialisation. This was necessary because neither individuals nor banks could accumulate the capital required to industrialise Sweden (Magnusson, 2005). The institutional change that enabled the industrial revolution in Sweden began in the 1840s. The guilds were abolished in 1846 and two years later the first limited liability company law was added. In the following decades, many and far-reaching changes in legislation were implemented which created a freer and more dynamic business life where trade, industry, and entrepreneurship could develop. Through the 1864 reforms, a general freedom of business was introduced for all men and unmarried women. The new regulations for trade, factory and craft contributed to stimulating entrepreneurship and growth throughout Sweden. During this period, the regulations that limited the banks' deposit and lending rates and prevented the establishment of limited companies were also abolished. The deregulation of the financial market facilitated new investments in industry and commerce (Andersson-Skoog & Magnusson, 2014). However, the Business Freedom Ordinance of 1864 did not only facilitate business freedom for the natives, but it also discriminated immigrant entrepreneurs from operating in Sweden (Nordlund, 1999a). One possible explanation for this may be that Sweden started to experience an emigration of young, able-bodied persons (especially to North America), an emigration-boom which culminated in the 1880s (Svanberg & Tydén, 1992). To pursue with the industrial development, the Swedish trade and industry needed labour. Seen from this perspective, it was more important to import workers than wealthy entrepreneurs (Nordlund, 1999a).

The Business Freedom Ordinance that was introduced in 1864 did not put an end to foreign ownership or foreign investments in Sweden, rather it changed the nature of ownership and investments. The new limited liability company act made it possible for foreigners to both own companies and invest in Sweden (Nordlund, 1989; Jörberg, 1988). Furthermore, it was possible for immigrants to start a company together with Swedish partners or to start a company after becoming a Swedish citizen (Nordlund, 1999a). Through joint stock companies, however, it was possible to accumulate the amount of capital required to build and operate such large production units that provided economies of scale in production and profit for the owners. During the pre-industrial era, not as much capital was required to build and run a small-scale industrial operation.

In the decades after World War II, Sweden experienced strong economic growth, which led to a shortage of labour in industry (Schön, 2000). This led to several important institutional changes. In 1954, a common Nordic labour market was introduced, which meant that no work permits or visas were needed to pick up a job in another Nordic country. This fed the Swedish labour market with much needed labour, especially from Finland (Fischer & Straubhaar, 1996). Furthermore, a collective labour transfer of Germans expelled from Eastern Europe who were in refugee camps in Austria and what later became the Federal Republic of Germany was organised (Tempsch, 1997). Sweden also concluded agreements with, for example, Yugoslavia, Greece, and Turkey on visa freedom to make it easier for workers from these countries to take up employment in Swedish industry (Rauhut, 2014). When Swedish industry could have its demand for labour satisfied, immigrant entrepreneurship no longer needed to be prevented or discouraged.

During the 1960s and 1970s, society came to change in a way that changed business and the view of business. The service sector overtook the industrial sector as the driving force in the Swedish economy in the mid-1960s (Schön, 2000). The industrial sector had mass-produced standardised products at a low price. Fordism constituted the main form of organisation. With the expansion of the service sector, much changed. Production was customised and information intensive. A mass production of standardised services in large production facilities does not work as much of the services are in demand on a local level (Magnusson, 2006). Technological and organisational changes, together with changing consumption patterns changed the conditions for entrepreneurship (Schön,

2000).[1] To this can be added an increased international division of labour and globalisation, which to some extent eliminated the Swedish industrial sectors that attracted the most labour immigrants during the 1950s and 1960s (Magnusson, 2002). During the 1970s and 1980s, immigrants had difficulty establishing themselves in the Swedish labour market (Lundh & Ohlsson, 1994a).

During the 1990s, Sweden was still one of the countries in the world with one of the smallest small business sectors in Western Europe and the capitalist world (Magnusson, 2006). In the early 1990s, there was a lack of planning, focus and collaboration with small business owners in most Swedish municipalities. Statistics on small businesses and self-employment first began to be kept in the early 1990s. The *explosion* of immigrant entrepreneurship that Sweden experienced during the 1990s may to some extent be a statistical illusion because statistics going back in time are missing (Nordlund, 1999b).

Sweden's EU membership meant a significant institutional change for Sweden when it comes to immigrant entrepreneurship. With few exceptions, EU citizens were legally equated with Swedes. Immigrants now comprised the group of non-EU citizens. An overwhelming majority of those who were previously classified as immigrants now received a new legal status and were legally equated with Swedes. The EU's free movement of services, goods, capital and labour in the internal market meant that Sweden had to change its regulations regarding companies and entrepreneurship, something which created opportunities for entrepreneurship among the EU citizens in Sweden. Furthermore, there were hopes that their increased entrepreneurship would increase the employment rate among immigrants. In a sense, EU citizens who established companies in Sweden became *privileged* immigrant entrepreneurs compared to their non-EU counterparts, as they operated under different conditions.

The Swedish EU membership is not the only institutional change taking place with an impact on immigrant entrepreneurship. Notably, in 2008, Sweden implemented one of the most liberal immigration policies among OECD countries. A key feature of this new immigration law was its provision allowing third-country nationals to immigrate specifically for the purpose of establishing their own businesses (OECD, 2011). This

[1] In fact, the entire conditions on the labour market changed during the 1970s and 1980s due to these changes. During the 1990s, the institutional framework for the Swedish labour market experienced significant changes. For more details, see Lundh (2000).

reform resulted in an approximate 10 percent increase in income among self-employed immigrants. This increase can be attributed to a process of self-selection among immigrant entrepreneurs and the market's comparatively greater reward for these new immigrant entrepreneurs than for earlier cohorts (Kazlou & Klinthäll, 2019).

To understand the mechanisms behind this enhanced market reward, it is crucial to note that most entrepreneurship visas were granted to individuals from the Middle East and Africa. These entrepreneurs predominantly established businesses within low-skilled service sectors and tended to concentrate in Sweden's three metropolitan regions, thereby forming ethnic enclaves (Kazlou & Urban, 2023). While the liberalisation of Swedish immigration policy undeniably contributed to income growth among immigrant entrepreneurs, the 'market reward' that Kazlou and Klinthäll (2019) identify simultaneously conceals rising segregation and the proliferation of parallel societies alongside the Swedish mainstream. Specifically, the increased stock of immigrants, i.e., non-EU citizens, has led to greater demand for immigrant-oriented products, resulting in higher incomes for those who can effectively cater to this demand.

Another crucial institutional dimension of immigrant entrepreneurship pertains to its role in the immigrant integration process. Evansluong (2016) posits that immigrant entrepreneurship can be understood as a dual integration mechanism, facilitating both the local incorporation of immigrant entrepreneurs into the host country and their reintegration into their country of origin. However, the extent to which immigrant entrepreneurship fosters integration is contingent on the individual immigrant's willingness to engage with the native population. For example, Engbersen et al. (2006) examined the formation and utilisation of social networks among different immigrant groups in Rotterdam, demonstrating that certain integration patterns cannot be adequately explained through the structural violence approach. Their study found that Turkish and Moroccan immigrants often developed dense yet relatively insular ethnic networks, defined as bonding social capital, whereas Surinamese and Antillean immigrants typically established more diverse networks that included connections with native Dutch residents, classified as bridging social capital. These distinctions in network formation significantly influenced integration outcomes, with immigrants possessing more bridging connections achieving better integration despite facing comparable structural conditions.

Applying the findings of Engbersen et al. (2006) to the Swedish case yields an important conclusion: if market incentives predominantly favour bonding rather than bridging social capital, immigrant entrepreneurship will prioritise serving the existing immigrant population, as suggested by Kazlou and Klinthäll (2019). This dynamic contradicts Evansluong's (2016) first assertion that immigrant entrepreneurship necessarily promotes integration. Instead, an emphasis on bonding social capital will reinforce immigrant entrepreneurs' reintegration into their countries of origin, which is in line with Evansluong's (2016) second argument. These entrepreneurs will effectively function as transnational conduits, linking their homeland with the diaspora community in Sweden. While the liberalisation of Sweden's immigration policy has undeniably stimulated immigrant entrepreneurship, it has not automatically facilitated the broader integration of the immigrant population into Swedish society.

4.5 Summary

During the Middle Ages, foreign entrepreneurs, mainly Germans, operated in the economically important Swedish cities such as Stockholm, Visby, Kalmar, and Söderköping. Their significant presence led to limitations on their political influence. During the mercantilist era and into the late nineteenth century, cities like Gothenburg, Stockholm, and Norrköping attracted foreign entrepreneurs. Immigrant refugees often started businesses after becoming Swedish citizens or partnering with native Swedes, especially in Gothenburg, a major immigration hub until World War II.

After World War II, immigration shifted towards labour until the late 1960s and refugees from the early 1970s, concentrating in metropolitan areas. Middle Eastern refugees today, often in ethnic enclaves, are prone to self-employment, producing services for their compatriots. Most contemporary immigrant entrepreneurship occurs in larger cities.

Historically, assessing the economic impact of immigrant entrepreneurship is challenging due to fragmented data. However, immigrants have introduced new ideas, products, and services. While some ventures succeeded quickly, others had limited impact. Foreign entrepreneurs played a significant role, attracting capital and opening new export destinations. The 1864 Business Freedom Ordinance facilitated foreign investment but limited the economic importance of immigrant entrepreneurs until the late 1960s. Post-WWII, Sweden sought labour migrants more than entrepreneurs, and the 1864 ordinance hindered immigrant entrepreneurship until its dismantling in 1968. EU membership in 1995 further removed obstacles for immigrant entrepreneurship.

Socially, Sweden was multi-ethnic until the nineteenth century, with Germans, Danes, Finns, Estonians, and others integrating through shared values and intermarriage. Conflicts occasionally arose, particularly with German merchants during the Middle Ages. In the nineteenth century, refugees, especially Jews from Eastern Europe, faced job difficulties, suspicion, and xenophobia. Post-World War II, labour immigrants from Nordic countries were welcomed, while refugees faced segregation and unemployment. Immigrant entrepreneurs experienced marginalisation, with many forming ethnic enclaves. The integration challenges resemble those faced by Eastern European Jews in the nineteenth century.

Regulations on immigrant entrepreneurship have evolved. During the Middle Ages and mercantilist era, wealthy immigrants were invited to stimulate economic development. In the 1840s, significant institutional changes, including abolishing guilds and introducing limited liability company laws, facilitated growth. The 1864 ordinance promoted business freedom for natives but discriminated against immigrant entrepreneurs. Post-World War II economic growth led to labour shortages and eased labour migration. By the mid-1960s, the service sector surpassed the industrial sector, and in the 1990s, immigrant entrepreneurship surged. Sweden's EU membership in 1995 aligned its legislation with the inner market, creating opportunities for immigrant entrepreneurs.

Lastly, it may be worth reflecting on to which extent the periodisation by Nordlund (1999a) is operationable and adequate. The main concern is if the periods between, on the one hand, the mid-1860s and World War II, and, on the other hand, the period between World War II and the mid-1990s can be considered two completely separated periods. The Business Freedom Ordinance of 1864, which had a most significant impact on immigrant entrepreneurship, was in rule until the late 1960s and after that a period of gradual dismantling of other obstacles for immigrant entrepreneurship were dismantled. The period between 1968, when the Business Freedom Ordinance of 1864 was shelved, up to the early 1990s marks a period of significant institutional change, which can be expected when an old and obsolete institutional framework is replaced with a new and dynamic one. The only difference between these two periods is that Jewish entrepreneurship was no longer discriminated after World War II. This criterion is not enough to consider these two periods as separate.

References

Andersson Joona, P. (2016). Integrationspolitiska insatser för nyanlända: Vilken roll spelar egenföretagandet? In J. Eklund (Ed.), *Swedish Economic Forum Report 2016: Immigration, ekonomisk integration och entreprenörskap* (pp. 54–73). Entreprenörskapsforum.

Andersson, M., Larsson, J. P., & Öner, Ö. (2021). Ethnic enclaves and self-employment among Middle Eastern immigrants in Sweden: Ethnic capital or enclave size? *Regional Studies, 55*(4), 590–604.

Andersson-Skoog, L., & Magnusson, L. (2014). Samhällsdynamik och industrialisering. In M. Larsson (red.), *Det svenska näringslivets historia 1864–2014* (pp. 14–197). Dialogos förlag.

Arnstberg, K.-O., & Ehn, B. (1976). *Etniska minoriteter förr och nu.* Liber läromedel.

Bäcklund, D. (1996). *Regionala skillnader i näringslivsstruktur 1840–1990.* Umeå Papers in Economic History no. 16.

Behre, G., Larsson, L. O., & Österberg, E. (1985). *Sveriges historia 1521–1809.* Esselte Studium.

Bevelander, P., Carlson, B., & Rojas, M. (1997). *I Krusbärslandets storstäder.* SNS förlag.

Broomé, P., Bäcklund, A. K., Lundh, C., & Ohlsson, R. (1998). *Varför sitter 'brassen' på bänken? Eller varför har invandrarna så svårt att få jobb?* SNS förlag.

Broström, L., & Rauhut, D. (2018). Poor men. On the masculinisation of poverty in Sweden 1957–1981. *Scandinavian Journal of History, 43*(3), 410–431.

Byström, M. (2006). *En broder, gäst och parasit. Uppfattningar och föreställningar om utlänningar, flyktingar och flyktingpolitik i svensk offentlig debatt 1942–1947.* PhD Thesis. Dept. of History, Stockholm University.

Carlson, B., & Hikam, A. (2016). Livlig aktivitet under ständigt hot—Somaliska företagare i Sydafrika. *Ekonomisk debatt, 44*(3), 14–25.

Carlson, B., & Schölin, T. (2016). *Etniskt företagande som startmotor.* Timbro.

Ekberg, J. (1977). Long-term effects of immigration. *Economy and History, 20*(1), 3–22.

Ekberg, J. (1999). Immigration and the public sector: Income effects for the native population in Sweden. *Journal Population Economics, 12*(3), 411–430.

Eklund, J. E., & Larsson, J. P. (2023). *Det nya utanförskapet.* Ekerlids förlag.

Engbersen, G., van der Leun, J., & de Boom, J. (2006). The fragmentation of migration and crime in the Netherlands. *Crime and Justice, 35*(1), 389–452.

Evansluong, Q. (2016). *Opportunity creation as a mixed embedding process: A study of immigrant entrepreneurs in Sweden.* PhD thesis, Jönköping International Business School.

Evansluong, Q., Ramirez Pasillas, M., & Nguyen Bergström, H. (2019). From breaking-ice to breaking-out: Integration as an opportunity creation process.

International Journal of Entrepreneurial Behaviour and Research, 25(5), 880–899.
Fischer, P. A., & Straubhaar, T. (1996). *Migration and economic integration in the Nordic Common Market*. Nordic Council of Ministers.
Gür, T., & Hellman. (1996). *En stjälpande hand—Om invandrarföretagares villkor i Sverige*. Ekonomifakta.
Gustafsson, B., & Österberg, T. (2001). Immigrants and the public sector budget—Accounting exercises for Sweden. *Journal Population Economics, 14*(4), 689–708.
Hammar, T. (1964). *Sverige åt svenskarna*. Doctoral Thesis, Department of Political Science, Stockholm University.
Heckscher, E. F. (1936). *Sveriges ekonomiska historia* (Vol. I:2). Bonniers.
Heckscher, E. F. (1949). *Sveriges ekonomiska historia* (Vol. II:1). Bonniers.
Heckscher, E. F. (1963). *Svenskt arbete och liv*. Aldus.
Johansson, M., & Rauhut, D. (2008). Invandrarnas bosättningsmönster i ett regionalt perspektiv 1950–2005. In G. Cars & C. J. Engström (Eds.), *Stadsregioners utvecklingskraft—Trender och nya perspektiv* (pp. 39–54). KTH.
Jörberg, L. (1988). *Svenska företagare under industrialismens genombrott 1870–1885*. Lund University Press.
Kazlou, A., & Klinthäll, M. (2019). Entrepreneurial response to changing opportunity structures: Self-selection and incomes among new immigrant entrepreneurs in Sweden. *International Journal of Entrepreneurial Behavior & Research, 25*(5), 859–879.
Kazlou, A., & Urban, S. (2023). Swedish migration policy liberalization and new immigrant entrepreneurs. *International Migration, 61*(2), 87–106.
Lindkvist, T., & Ågren, K. (1985). *Sveriges medeltid*. Norstedts.
Lundh, C. (2000). *Spelets regler. Institutioner och lönebildning på den svenska arbetsmarknaden 1850–2000*. SNS förlag.
Lundh, C., & Ohlsson, R. (1992). *Från arbetskraftsimport till flyktinginvandring*. SNS förlag.
Lundh, C., & Ohlsson, R. (1994a). *Från arbetskraftsimport till flyktinginvandring*. SNS förlag.
Lundh, C., & Ohlsson, R. (1994b). Immigration and economic change. In T. Bengtsson (Ed.), *Population, economy, and welfare in Sweden* (pp. 87–107). Springer.
Magnusson, L. (1999). *Merkantilism. Ett ekonomiskt tänkande formuleras*. SNS förlag.
Magnusson, L. (2002). *Sveriges ekonomiska historia*. Prisma.
Magnusson, L. (2005). *Den synliga handen. Nation, stat och det industriella bygget*. SNS förlag.
Magnusson, L. (2006). *Den tredje industriella revolutionen*. Norstedts akademiska förlag.

Nordlund, S. (1989). *Upptäckten av Sverige. Utländska direktinvesteringar i Sverige 1895–1945.* Umeå Studies in Economic History no. 12. Department of Economic History, Umeå University.

Nordlund, S. (1999a). Invandrarföretagande i Sverige—En historisk tillbakablick. In Kulturdepartementet, *Invandrare som företagare*, SOU 1999:49 (pp. 354–364). Regeringskansliet.

Nordlund, S. (1999b). Kommentarer eller synpunkter rörande insatser för att åstadkomma lika behandling av rörelseidkare oavsett etnisk och kulturell bakgrund. In Kulturdepartementet, *Invandrare som företagare*, SOU 1999:49 (pp. 346–353). Regeringskansliet.

NUTEK. (2001). *Marginalisering eller integration—Invandrares företagande i svensk retorik och praktik.* Nutek.

OECD. (2011). *Recruiting immigrant workers: Sweden 2011.* Retrieved May 13, 2025, from https://www.oecd.org/en/publications/recruiting-immigrant-workers-sweden-2011_9789264167216-en.html

Ohlsson, H., Broomé, P., & Bevelander, P. (2012). Self-employment of immigrants and natives in Sweden—A multilevel analysis. *Entrepreneurship and Regional Development, 24*(5–6), 405–423.

Rauhut, D. (2014). *I moder Sveas ömma famn.* Carlsons bokförlag.

Rauhut, D. (2019a). Arbetskraftsinvandringens drivkrafter 1945–1960—En problematisering och kritik. In D. Rauhut & L. Broström (red.), *Med öppna armar? Om integration och invandring till Sverige 1945–1970* (pp. 205–229). Daidalos.

Rauhut, D. (2019b). Sverige, invandrarna och integrationen 1947–1967. In D. Rauhut & L. Broström (red.), *Med öppna armar? Om integration och invandring till Sverige 1945–1970* (pp. 141–162). Daidalos.

Rauhut, D. (2020). Integration and informal institutions. *Society, 57*(2), 211–218.

Rauhut, D., & Laine, J. (2023). Crossing the border: Immigrant integration in a bordering perspective. In D. Rauhut (Ed.), *New methods and theory on immigrant integration: Insights from remote and peripheral areas* (pp. 68–55). Edward Elgar.

Rauhut, D., & Rauhut Kompaniets, O. (2018). The impact of immigrant entrepreneurship regional development in Western Sweden. *Romanian Journal of Regional Science, 12*(1), 18–42.

Rauhut, D., Aigner-Walder, B., & Schomaker, R. (2022). *The economics of immigration beyond the cities: Theoretical perspectives and empirical insights.* Palgrave Macmillan.

Schön, L. (2000). *En modern svensk ekonomisk historia.* SNS förlag.

Svanberg, I., & Tydén, M. (1992). *Tusen år av invandring.* Gidlunds bokförlag.

Tempsch, R. (1997). *Från Centraleuropa till Folkhemmet: Den sudet-tyska invandringen till Sverige 1938–1955.* Meddelanden från Ekonomisk-historiska institutionen vid Göteborgs universitet, nr. 73. PhD Thesis, Gothenburg University.

CHAPTER 5

The Swedish Scholarship on Immigrant Entrepreneurship

Abstract The discussion in this chapter focuses on how immigrant entrepreneurship has been handled in Swedish research, why immigrants have become entrepreneurs, and what discourses the research has taken place in. It also identifies some areas where there are research gaps to fill.

Keywords Research discourse • Motivations • Policy • Spatial dynamics • Institutional change

This chapter discusses the evolving landscape of research on immigrant entrepreneurship, highlighting significant shifts and trends over time. The discussion is structured around three pivotal aspects: (1) the discourse surrounding the research, (2) the specific focus areas within the field of immigrant entrepreneurship, and (3) the key findings that have emerged. Initially, the section will explore the discourse of immigrant entrepreneurship in Sweden, examining how academic and policy narratives have framed the phenomenon. By understanding the discourse, we can gain insights into how immigrant entrepreneurship has been perceived and studied over different periods. Following this, the discussion will shift to the focus areas of research on immigrant entrepreneurship. This part will scrutinise the various dimensions that scholars have concentrated on, such as the socio-economic backgrounds of immigrant entrepreneurs, the types

D. Rauhut, *Immigrant Entrepreneurship in Sweden*,
https://doi.org/10.1007/978-3-032-02466-4_5

of businesses they establish, and the challenges and opportunities they encounter.

The third aspect of the discussion will address the findings of research on immigrant entrepreneurship. Here, we will summarise the key outcomes of empirical studies, highlighting patterns and trends in immigrant entrepreneurial activities. This includes examining the motivations behind why immigrants choose to become entrepreneurs in Sweden, the sectors they are most active in, and the success factors and barriers they face. When this is done, the role of policy incentives designed to stimulate immigrant entrepreneurship will be analysed, assessing their effectiveness and impact. The focus will be on contemporary policy measures. The chapter will conclude with a comprehensive summary, synthesising the main points discussed and offering reflections on the future directions of research in this field.

5.1 The Discourse of Immigrant Entrepreneurship

Two main discourses had an impact on why immigrant entrepreneurship suddenly became a research area in the 1990s. While one relates to the structural change of the Swedish economy and the impact this has had on the demand for labour, the other relates to a changing political rhetoric and ideological preferences.

5.1.1 Structural Change and Labour Market Demands

The first discourse relates to the challenges immigrants have had to establish themselves on the Swedish labour market since the early 1970s. Changes in, among other things, technology and work organisation led to employers gradually demanding different skills during the 1970s and 1980s than during the 1950s and 1960s. This has meant that the immigrants' labour supply in most cases does not match the employers' demand for labour, which is related to the new skill requirements. This mainly applies to proficiency in the Swedish language and other communicative skills, social competence and requirements for a theoretical education (Broomé et al., 1998). From the end of World War II until the end of the 1960s, the immigration of labour from the Nordic countries and Europe dominated, and these immigrants came mainly for unskilled work in Swedish industry (Lundh & Ohlsson, 1994). At most, refugees made up

25 percent of immigrants during this period (Rauhut, 2014).[1] They had no problems getting work in the industrial sector as the jobs were unskilled (Ohlsson, 1978). Since the 1970s, immigration to Sweden has mainly consisted of refugees from countries outside Europe (Lundh & Ohlsson, 1994). A lower level of education and lack of language skills have made it increasingly difficult for non-European immigrants to find work in Sweden (Lundh et al., 2002; Åslund et al., 2006). Based on register data on all persons who arrived in Sweden in each of the years 1990, 1994, 1998, and 2002 the findings suggest that it takes *on average* 17 years for immigrants from middle- and low-income countries to obtain a consecutive employment on 12 months (Gustafsson et al., 2017). The difficulties for immigrants to get a foothold on the Swedish labour market has slowly deteriorated since the mid-1970s. The gap between immigrants and natives regarding e.g., employment rates, educational levels and incomes increased between 1975 and 1995 (for an overview, see Häll, 1997). Most refugees arriving in Sweden lack the requisite human capital to be competitive in the Swedish labour market. Therefore, significant investments in their education are essential for enhancing their competitiveness (Rauhut, 2004).

To understand the width of the challenges related to problems to get established on the labour market it is needed to examine what 'language proficiency' and 'lacking competence' hide. While less than 9 percent of the Swedish population has primary school education (including less than primary school education and primary school dropouts) as highest educational attainment level in 2019, the corresponding share of the Third Country National (i.e., non-EU immigrants) was about 34 percent. In some Swedish regions, the share of Third Country Nationals with such low educational attainment level almost reached 60 percent (Rauhut et al., 2023). In the international survey conducted by the Program for International Assessment of Adult Competencies (PIAAC) in 2013 on the reading comprehension, numeracy and problem-solving skills of the adult population, it was found that approximately 13 percent of the total Swedish adult population did not have sufficient reading skills. This corresponds to approximately 780,000 people aged 16 to 65 (SCB, 2015).

[1] In sources from the 1950s and 1960s, the Germans who were transferred from refugee camps in Germany and Austria were considered refugees. In the 1990s, the very same migrants are classified as labour migrants (Tempsch, 1997). If the Germans who came to Sweden via refugee camps are classified as refugees, the share of refugees to Sweden 1945–1970 is approximately 25 percent (Rauhut, 2014).

> Taken as a whole, those born abroad are heavily overrepresented in the very weakest group, i.e. those who have major problems in both reading and arithmetic skills. There are many here who have immigrated to Sweden in recent years and do not yet have sufficient knowledge of the Swedish language. /…/ Just over 35 percent of people born outside Sweden show insufficient skills in both areas of knowledge, compared to about 5 percent among those born in the country. (SCB, 2015, pp. 22–23. Own translation)

When the PIAAC was conducted again in 2023, the findings showed only marginal changes; the significant gap between natives and immigrants persists. However, the 2023 evaluation notes that the skills in reading comprehension, numeracy, and problem-solving among the adult immigrant population vary considerably. Those with tertiary education displayed high scores in the 2023 PIAAC test, whereas those with only primary education scored low (SCB, 2024).

In a knowledge-intensive service economy, such as the Swedish, the gap in formal competences and language proficiency poses serious obstacles for immigrants to enter the labour market. It is of outmost importance to address these two areas politically (Andersson Joona, 2019; Åslund et al., 2006. See also Nordström Skans & Åslund, 2009).

5.1.2 The Postcolonial Narrative

The second discourse of relevance relates to political rhetoric and ideological preferences. In the late 1980s and early 1990s, there was much frustration about immigrants' lack of integration into the Swedish society. The Social Democrats proposed a new bill on how to make immigrants adjust into the Swedish society in 1991, but after the centre-right coalition won the parliament election the same year, the bill was shelved. Instead, a new commission to investigate how immigrants could better adjust to the Swedish society was appointed. This commission was dissolved when the Social Democrats returned to office in 1994. Instead, a new commission was appointed, and it presented its report on how immigrants could be better integrated in Sweden in 1996. The key takeaway from the bill that was proposed in 1997 is that immigrants were expected to follow Swedish legislation and be able to communicate in Swedish after an introduction period (Dahlström, 2004).

Inspired by postcolonialism, the immigration policy pursued was criticised as inherently discriminatory. The immigrant must submit to Swedish solely because the person is an immigrant and they are blamed because of their culture, a culture which they otherwise have the right to practise (Dahlström, 2004). The criticism during the 1990s against the pursued policy rather gives expression to exploiting the immigrants, oppressing them and subjecting the immigrants to unfair treatment. Issues relating to the distribution of power and distribution of economic resources between Swedes and immigrants are not touched upon in the integration policy, and as long as these are not included, the situation of the immigrants will not change. The immigrants are thus exposed to structural violence in that they have been racialised (Molina, 1997).

In the postcolonial narrative, Sweden is described as a deeply racist country where immigrants are racialised, discriminated against, and exploited (Mattsson & Tesfahuney, 2002; Catomeris, 2002; Bunar, 2002; de los Reyes, 2002). Furthermore, the immigrants' problems establishing themselves in, e.g., the labour and housing markets are attributed to an inherent racism in Swedish society (Mulinari, 2002; Andersson, 2002; Neergaard, 2002). If the situation of immigrants is to change, a redistribution of power in Sweden must take place (Dahlstedt, 2002). Capitalism is based on the marginalised poor and immigrants who can be exploited (Amin, 2002). The criticism can be summarised as follows:

> The requirements to adapt to Swedish legislation and to use Swedish in the dominated majority society can be regarded as different forms of functional integration. It is simply a demand for the least possible degree of adaptation, which in other words is a demand for assimilation. It is difficult to disregard a requirement for individuals to refrain from practicing parts of the home country's traditions, as well as stated or unstated requirements for Swedish as a means of communication, which are also assimilation requirements, i.e. the adaptation of the minorities to the surrounding society. (Popoola, 2002, p. 25. Own translation)

Influenced by the left-wing criticism directed at the alleged return to a policy that was mainly based on assimilation, in 2000 the social democratic government appointed a commission to investigate the situation of immigrants in Swedish society, and the inquiry was led by postcolonial researchers (Lindgren, 2022). When the commission report was handed over to the responsible minister in 2006, it ended up in the bin. In many ways, the commission dealt with ideology production rather than seriously conducted research aimed at serving as a basis for political decision-making (Widmalm, 2019).

Up to the 1990s, immigration and integration policy had been very consensus-oriented in the Swedish parliament (Dahlström, 2004). The most important consequence of the criticism that postcolonial researchers directed at the consensus-like integration policy since the early 1990s is probably that the immigration and integration policies have become politicised. Thereby these policy areas have become part of the *culture war* that is still raging on how to impose one's own ideology (beliefs, virtues, and practices) on the Swedish society (Widmalm, 2019; Heinö Johansson, 2021).[2]

The postcolonial narrative is also present in research on immigrant entrepreneurship. The fundamental premise is that immigrants experience systematic discrimination, making self-employment the only viable means of livelihood. As entrepreneurs, they continue to face discrimination from various actors, such as financiers and customers (see Evansluong, 2016; Evansluong et al., 2019; Kazlou, 2019; Zalkat, 2024).

5.2 The Motivations for Immigrant Entrepreneurship

Before the Business Freedom Ordinance of 1864, foreigners were *invited* and encouraged to start and operate businesses in Sweden. They were often granted privileges such as monopoly markets, legal freedoms, tax breaks, and the right to practise their religion, and these privileges effectively acted as drivers to reallocate and become an entrepreneur in Sweden. Jewish entrepreneurs received special privileges to attract them to Sweden (Nordlund, 1999a). However, the privileged position of Jews began to be dismantled in 1938. Moreover, during the latter half of the nineteenth century, anti-Jewish sentiments were widespread (Svanberg & Tydén, 1992). The Business Freedom Ordinance of 1864 restricted the opportunities for foreigners to establish companies as sole proprietorships and partnerships (Nordlund, 1999a). Foreign ownership in Swedish limited

[2] A *culture war* serves as a metaphor for contentious politics centred around values and ideologies. It manifests through deliberately adversarial social narratives, aiming to incite political polarisation within mainstream society. These narratives focus on both economic matters of public policy (Hartman, 2015) and consumption (Diaz Ruiz & Nilsson, 2022). In practical terms, culture wars revolve around social issues rooted in abstract discussions about values, morality, and lifestyle. Their purpose is to create political divisions in multicultural societies (Koleva et al., 2012).

liability companies and stock market companies was permitted but regulated by separate legislation (Nordlund, 1989).

Leaving the historical perspective and focusing on the contemporary explanations, research around small businesses and entrepreneurship has identified three main groups of motives for an individual to start a business. It is about causal explanations at different levels (Eriksson & Larsson, 2001):

- *Structural/cyclical reasons.* This reason is largely about factors such as employment and unemployment. Furthermore, it comes into play that the conditions for starting a business in a service-producing economy are more favourable than in an economy dominated by industrial production.
- *Institutional reasons.* A trend in business is related to more and more activities being outsourced, that is, more and more companies are buying services on a contract basis instead of producing them themselves. Also tax system, pension legislation, rules for labour immigration, etc. influence the decision to start a business.
- *Individual causes.* The individual reasons can be divided into two main groups: objective motives (e.g., gender, age, ethnicity, education, professional experience and family background) and experiential motives (e.g., search for independence or dissatisfaction in the workplace).

In addition to the three primary groups, there are individuals who identify a unique business idea and feel compelled to bring it to fruition. An unmet need in the market serves as another impetus for starting a business (Henreksson & Stenkula, 2007). Research also highlights the significance of professional experience within established organisations before embarking on an entrepreneurial journey (Rider et al., 2013, p. 31). It is reasonable to assume that this experience enables individuals to identify unmet needs in specific markets and equips them with the knowledge to address those needs effectively.

When examining the key motivations behind starting a business, three factors stand out: (1) a desire for independence (Skaug, 2000), (2) recognition of an unfulfilled market need, and (3) unemployment (Henreksson & Stenkula, 2007). It is possible to establish a connection between these three primary motivations and the reasons why individuals with foreign backgrounds initiate businesses in Sweden, allowing us to draw meaningful conclusions. To consider *independence* as a primary motivation for individuals with a foreign background to start a company, we assume that they are already successfully integrated into the Swedish labour market before venturing into entrepreneurship. However, given that the employment rate for people with a foreign background is lower than that for natives, and the unemployment rate is higher, it is reasonable to conclude that while independence may drive some foreign-background entrepreneurs, it is not universally applicable. Additionally, the motivation of addressing an *unmet market need* relies on experience and knowledge, which many individuals with a foreign background lack due to their limited presence in the Swedish labour market. Nevertheless, for those who have established themselves, this motive remains significant (Rauhut et al., 2014). Among individuals with a foreign background, *unemployment* emerges as the primary impetus for starting businesses (Aronsson, 1991; Hout & Rosen, 1999; Eriksson & Larsson, 2001; Klinthäll et al., 2016).

No doubt, immigrants and refugees have experienced discrimination, racism and economic segregation in Sweden, which have made it difficult to enter the regular labour market (Åslund et al., 2006; Klinthäll et al., 2016). However, it must also be emphasised that low educational attainment levels, a poor proficiency in the Swedish language and, generally, a low demand for unqualified labour in the knowledge-intensive Swedish economy do not help immigrants in general and refugees in particular to establish themselves at the labour market. At the same time, immigrants with a good language proficiency in Swedish, cultural knowledge and with a competitive education do well as entrepreneurs in Sweden (Backman et al., 2021). Although it may play a role for the impetus for starting businesses, the gap between actual discrimination and racism versus the self-perceived discrimination and racism appear not to have been discussed in Sweden. With a low education and poor language skills, it is possible to blame discrimination and racism. The main problem, however, is that the labour offered at the regular labour market is not competitive; employers demand labour with, generally speaking, a higher human capital (Aldén & Hammarstedt, 2015). The study by Backman et al. (2021, p. 980) concludes that 'over one-third of refugees followed a "less successful" pathway, characterized by a consistent long period of inactivity in the educational system and labor market'. The share of 'less successful' refugees on the labour market is about the same share as those non-EU with primary education as the highest educational attainment level (Rauhut et al., 2023) and those with very low proficiency in the Swedish language as well as in numeracy (SCB, 2015). This correlation has been discussed in previous research (Åslund et al., 2006. See also Nordström Skans & Åslund, 2009). When such high share of the non-EU citizens is unable to provide for themselves, the result in housing district struggling with e.g., distress, social exclusion, and high criminality may not come as a surprise (Eklund & Larsson, 2023).

The research focus on policies on immigrant entrepreneurship in Sweden has been to stimulate self-employment and entrepreneurship as an alternative to unemployment (see e.g., Kazlou & Urban, 2023; Åslund et al., 2006; Aldén & Hammarstedt, 2015; Klinthäll et al., 2016). In other words, entrepreneurship has become a labour market instrument. Moreover, it is worth noting that several studies focus on the potential of immigrant entrepreneurship and not on the actual performance (Wennberg & Efendic, 2013; Carlson & Schölin, 2016). No doubt that immigrant entrepreneurship can be beneficial—both for the entrepreneur and for the society. However, success or failure when it comes to entrepreneurship is partly related to what policies there are to promote and stimulate entrepreneurship.

5.3 Refugee Entrepreneurship

While research on immigrant entrepreneurship has been extensive, the focus on refugee entrepreneurship is a relatively new phenomenon. Few studies address refugees' entrepreneurial decisions and actions (Abebe, 2019, 2023), as well as their motivations, challenges, and experiences (Embiricos, 2020). The lack of empirically based knowledge on refugee entrepreneurship is even more pronounced in Sweden. Historically, the scarcity of empirical research led stakeholders to rely on literature regarding immigrant entrepreneurship (Bevelander, 2011; Ruist, 2015). Although this approach assumes that refugees and non-refugee immigrants share similar drivers and challenges, it is a bold assumption. The limited research points at differences between refugees and labour migrants (Zalkat, 2024). Labour migrants generally migrate for economic and social improvement, often with prearranged employment, whereas refugees flee involuntarily due to war, political or religious violence, persecution, or natural disasters (OECD, 2019).

Empirical research on entrepreneurship among immigrants and refugees in Sweden is relatively recent. While immigrants could start joint stock companies and be entrepreneurial in the late nineteenth and early twentieth centuries (Nordlund, 1989), refugees faced discrimination when attempting to establish partnerships or sole proprietorships under the Business Freedom Ordinance of 1864 (Svanberg & Tydén, 1992). Current research highlights the discrimination refugees encounter when trying to start businesses (e.g., Zalkat, 2024; Akhtar, 2024; Slavnik, 2013), while labour migrants and researchers involved in high-growth potential ventures are more welcomed. The differential treatment of immigrants and refugees appears related to the type of business activity, whether it is labour-intensive and low-productive or capital-intensive and high-productive, and the corporate form of the entrepreneurship.

Refugee entrepreneurship is only a part of immigrant entrepreneurship. Legally, EU citizens are not considered immigrants; only non-EU citizens (Third Country Nationals) are. It is crucial to understand the performance of non-refugee immigrants from outside the EU as entrepreneurs in Sweden and their reasons for choosing Sweden. Since 2008, Sweden has offered a special visa for entrepreneurs (Kazlou & Urban, 2023). Asylum seekers can also start a business after submitting their application (Verksamt, 2024). However, if their asylum application is rejected, they cannot change their visa category unless they have been employed for four months and have a promise of continued employment for at least 12 months, allowing them to apply for a work permit or start a company (Tillväxtverket, 2017). Most 'entrepreneurship' visas have been granted to individuals from the Middle East and Africa, who typically start companies in low-skilled service sectors (Kazlou & Urban, 2023). In conclusion, the majority of 'entrepreneurship visas' for immigrants from outside the EU seem to be related to refugees and refugee entrepreneurship.

5.4 The Spatial Dimension

Historically, immigrant entrepreneurs have predominantly operated in Sweden's major cities, as discussed in Chap. 4, Stockholm has always been a key city. During the Middle Ages, the most important cities were Stockholm, Visby, Kalmar, and Söderköping (Lindkvist & Ågren, 1985). In the Mercantilist Era, cities like Stockholm, Gothenburg, Norrköping, Karlskrona, and Eskilstuna became centres of immigrant entrepreneurship (Heckscher, 1949). From the late nineteenth century up to World War II, cities such as Stockholm, Gothenburg, Borås, Landskrona, Motala, Malmö, Örebro, and Sundsvall had the highest numbers of immigrant entrepreneurs. Gothenburg served as the gateway city for immigration during this period (Svanberg & Tydén, 1992). In the post-war era, immigrants have generally clustered in the three metropolitan areas around Stockholm, Gothenburg, and Malmö (Rauhut, 2014). These areas continue to host most immigrant entrepreneurs (Nordlund, 1999a).

Several studies show that ethnic enclaves increase the propensity for immigrant entrepreneurship and self-employment. Immigrants in these enclaves provide goods and services to their co-ethnics that Swedish natives cannot (Andersson & Hammarstedt, 2015; Andersson & Larsson, 2016; Andersson et al., 2021; Ohlsson et al., 2012; Tavassoli & Trippl, 2019). Ethnic enclaves are common in Sweden's three metropolitan regions and in larger cities with populations between 100,000 and 300,000. In rural and remote areas, ethnic enclaves are less common and smaller if they exist (Kazlou & Urban, 2023; Hårsman, 2006; Rauhut et al., 2023).

Kordel and Weidinger (2018) conclude that despite high expectations from local stakeholders for demographic stabilisation and labour shortage mitigation, there is little evidence of refugee integration in rural employment markets. Refugees are often pushed into self-employment for survival. Bansak et al. (2021) note that host countries often disperse refugees to minimise impacts, placing them in economically depressed regions with few other immigrants, making it difficult for them to succeed and access migrant networks that aid in transitioning. Rauhut et al. (2023) find a negative correlation between the share of non-EU citizens and company startups in regions beyond cities in Europe, indicating insufficient demand for the ethnic enclave economy in these areas.

Indirect factors impacting immigrant entrepreneurship include the increasing share of population in working ages in peripheral localities and the negative relationship between the foreign population share and the ageing profile of a place in Sweden (Backman & Karlsson, 2024). This paradoxically reduces labour demand (Mitze et al., 2018), which in turn lowers aggregate demand for goods and services, making entrepreneurship less profitable for both immigrants and natives in these regions (Rauhut et al., 2023).

5.5 The Role of Immigrant Entrepreneurship

Sweden remained a poor and underdeveloped country on the European periphery for long. The nation's economy was predominantly agrarian, plagued by chronic shortages of capital, knowledge, technology, and skilled labour. To address these challenges, attracting skilled, capital-strong, and ambitious entrepreneurs from other countries became a viable strategy (Behre et al., 1985; Berend & Ranki, 1982). German merchants and craftsmen played a significant role during this period, contributing their capital and connections to tie Sweden more closely to the markets of medieval Europe. Consequently, they had lasting economic effects on Swedish mining, urban industries, foreign trade, and overall economic growth (Heckscher, 1936). Inspired by mercantilist ideas, the Swedish state actively sought to attract knowledgeable foreigners during the seventeenth and eighteenth centuries. These foreigners were encouraged to engage in industrial and commercial ventures, exploiting and refining domestic resources for subsequent export. The overarching goal was to boost the country's income and enhance self-sufficiency. To entice these foreign entrepreneurs, the state granted privileges such as tax breaks, religious freedom, and legal rights (Heckscher, 1949; Magnusson, 1999).

The aim of immigrant entrepreneurship in Sweden prior to the introduction of the Business Freedom Ordinance of 1864 was to make up for shortages and deficits of capital, knowledge, technology, and skilled labour. Immigrant entrepreneurship was stimulated because it was used as a means to improve Sweden's economic capacity. To conclude, during the Middle Ages and the Mercantilist era, immigrant entrepreneurship served as a *supplementation* to deficient domestic entrepreneurship in terms of e.g., capital, knowledge, and technology.

The Business Freedom Ordinance of 1864 was discriminatory against some immigrants. Foreigners who wanted to start businesses in Sweden as stock companies or entered a partnership with native investors could do so, but refugees who wanted to start a small family business or a sole proprietorship encountered discriminatory obstacles. The business owner did not only have to show security for three years' taxes to the state and municipality, but also that he/she was of good morals and that his/her business produced an added value to Sweden. It was also important to show that the business did not compete with domestic business (Nordlund, 1999b). In other words, if the entrepreneurship was beneficial to Sweden it was allowed to start. Hence, entrepreneurship by foreigners, and especially by refugees, in the form of small family business or a sole proprietorship was allowed if they could show that they were *complementary* to domestic entrepreneurship. In sectors and industries where the entrepreneurship was competing with domestic entrepreneurs, the immigrant or refugee had to enter a company partnership with a native or wait until they became a Swedish citizen before they could start the company. The Business Freedom Ordinance of 1864 was not dismantled until the late 1960s.

Between 1960 and 1990, the share of immigrant-owned small businesses increased from approximately 3 percent to around 10 percent. Until the 1980s, only a small number of immigrant small business owners were non-Europeans. However, by 1990, every fourth small business was run by a non-European immigrant. These immigrant entrepreneurs found success in sectors such as e.g., hotels, restaurants, retail trade, and general services (Nordlund, 1999b). Notably, the income levels of immigrant small business owners were significantly lower than those of Swedish small business owners, suggesting that immigrant entrepreneurs often operated in less profitable sectors (Gustafsson et al., 1990). However, the expansion of immigrant entrepreneurship between 1960 and 1990 generally takes place when immigrants found it more difficult to get a foothold on the Swedish labour market.

In the 1990s, the outlook for immigrant entrepreneurship appears grim. These immigrants face marginalisation, which has shifted from unemployment exclusion to economic marginalisation within business (NUTEK, 2001). During the 2010s, Sweden received a substantial number of refugees relative to its population, primarily from Africa and Asia. However, integration into the Swedish labour market remains elusive, let alone integration into Swedish society (Eklund & Larsson, 2023). Many of these immigrants have formed clusters in suburban areas of large cities, creating ethnic enclaves (Edin et al., 2003; Hårsman, 2006). Within these enclaves, some immigrants have become entrepreneurs, offering goods and services to fellow compatriots (Andersson et al., 2021; Andersson & Hammarstedt, 2015; Andersson & Larsson, 2016; Hammarstedt, 2006). Immigrant entrepreneurship tends to concentrate in low-productivity, labour-intensive sectors with slim profit margins. Examples include restaurants, taxis, hairdressers, convenience stores, retail, cleaning companies, and personal services. Many of these industries are also sensitive to economic cycles (Rauhut & Rauhut Kompaniets, 2018). In conclusion, when labour lacks matching demand, entrepreneurship becomes an alternative source of livelihood. Most refugee entrepreneurs produce goods and services for their fellow compatriots within these ethnic enclaves. This kind of immigrant entrepreneurship is not a supplementation nor complementary to domestic entrepreneurship, rather it operates *parallel* to domestic entrepreneurship.

5.6 The Missing Aspect: Institutional Changes

Throughout this essay, one aspect with immigrant entrepreneurship appears troublesome. When does immigrant entrepreneurship occur and when does it not? According to the definition, discussed in Chap. 2, natives and EU-citizens are non-immigrants, and therefore cannot be considered immigrant entrepreneurs if they start a company, only non-EU citizens are immigrants. Entrepreneurship occurs when you start a company. Consequently, immigrant entrepreneurship takes place when non-EU citizens start a company. This is a simple and clear definition of immigrant entrepreneurship. However, we must include ***what kind*** of company the immigrants start (a sole proprietorship, a partnership, or a stock company with limited liability). *Ownership* and *control* over the company appear the keys here, and it is here it becomes troublesome.

If the company started is a sole proprietorship, or a partnership, the ownership and control of the company is obvious: the persons or person who started it is the owner and controls it. For small businesses that are stock companies with limited liability, the person or persons who founded it may have control over the company shares and hence control the company. Seen from a historical perspective, this is how immigrant entrepreneurship has worked since it started. Although foreign entrepreneurs were invited to Sweden to run their businesses, these entrepreneurs owned and controlled their companies. The Business Freedom Ordinance of 1864, started to discriminate this kind of immigrant entrepreneurship, and it continued to do so until the late 1960s. Services we utilise on a regular basis, such as e.g., hairdressers, restaurants, taxis, convenience stores etc., are generally run as a sole proprietorship, or a partnership. These industries are labour-intensive and low-productive, and, generally, they do struggle with slim profit margins. Still today, we find immigrants overrepresented as entrepreneurs in these industries, and they still struggle to accumulate the needed capital to start up their business. The point here, is that it is a simple operation to identify the ownership and control over these companies, and hence it is simple to identify which of them are immigrant companies and which is not.

This is not the case with bigger stock companies with limited liability. Let us assume that a non-EU citizen has a brilliant idea for a capital-intensive and high-productive company which can be assumed to grow for a significant period and will generate significant profits to the owners. In this example, we can assume that this company has the potential to become a leading actor at the global level in the industry it operates in. This non-EU citizen turns to all the forms of support described above and receives maximum support. A stock company is founded, with the non-EU citizen with the original idea being represented in the company board. Then there are representatives from all risk-capitalists who have invested in the company. The investors expect to get their money back, both through yields on their company shares but also by selling their shares in the company at a higher price than they bought them for. The key question here is if this is an immigrant company and an example of immigrant entrepreneurship. When looking at who controls and owns the company, it is obvious that it is not the person who had the original idea, i.e., the non-EU citizen.[3]

Looking back at the effect of the Business Freedom Ordinance of 1864, sole proprietorship was discriminated at, but not stock companies with foreign investors and owners. Nor were immigrants hindered to enter partnerships with natives; the company was then classified as native, and hence the Business Freedom Ordinance of 1864 did not discriminate them. Rather, it seems as if some forms of ownership and control were discriminated at, and not the immigrant. This is an aspect which future research needs to investigate further.

Another significant institutional change is the EU membership in 1995. Entrepreneurs who were citizens in EU Member States before Sweden entered the EU were considered immigrant entrepreneurs, but after Sweden became an EU Member State, the very same entrepreneurs stopped being immigrant entrepreneurs to turn non-immigrant entrepreneurs. To what extent entrepreneurs in Sweden who are EU citizens perform differently from natives or immigrant entrepreneurs is an area which has attracted little interest in Sweden. The same can be said about whether the sectors where EU citizens start companies differ from the sectors where native or immigrant entrepreneurs operate.

The liberalisation of Swedish immigration law in 2008 represents a significant institutional change in the context of immigrant entrepreneurship. As outlined in Chap. 4, while this reform may have contributed to the growth of immigrant entrepreneurship, it does not appear to have facilitated the integration of immigrants, as entrepreneurial activities have largely been directed towards serving other immigrants.

[3] If we, using the same example, swap the non-EU citizen for an EU-citizen, the company automatically becomes an example of a non-immigrant entrepreneurship.

5.7 Summary

Research on immigrant entrepreneurship in Sweden has gained attention since the 1990s, driven by structural economic changes and political rhetoric shifts. The primary research focuses on the challenges immigrants face in establishing themselves in the labour market, exacerbated by technological advancements and evolving work organisations. These changes created a mismatch between immigrants' skills and labour market demands, particularly in terms of Swedish language proficiency and theoretical education, making it harder for non-European immigrants to find employment. Additionally, postcolonial critiques argue that the integration policies of the 1990s are discriminatory, exploiting and oppressing immigrants, and call for a redistribution of power and economic resources.

Historically, foreign entrepreneurs in Sweden were attracted by privileges such as monopoly markets and tax breaks before the 1864 Business Freedom Ordinance, which revoked many of these advantages, particularly for Jewish entrepreneurs. Contemporary research identifies three main motives for starting a business: structural (employment/unemployment), institutional (outsourcing, tax systems), and individual (desire for independence, dissatisfaction at work). Immigrants in Sweden often pursue entrepreneurship to address unemployment and discrimination. Those with good language skills, cultural knowledge, and competitive education perform well, but many face significant barriers due to limited financial capital and bank discrimination.

Research on immigrant entrepreneurship has primarily focused on motivations, challenges, and support mechanisms. However, gaps remain in understanding the long-term impacts of integration policies, the effectiveness of targeted support, and the differences between various immigrant groups, such as refugees and non-EU citizens; EU citizens are not immigrants. Further research is needed to explore the role of institutional changes, the effects of EU membership, and the potential of public procurement to stimulate immigrant entrepreneurship. Additionally, examining the economic contributions of immigrant entrepreneurs in various sectors and their impact on local economies could provide valuable insights into improving support mechanisms and promoting sustainable business ventures for immigrants in Sweden.

In conclusion, while significant progress has been made in understanding immigrant entrepreneurship in Sweden, there are still many areas that require further investigation. Addressing these research gaps will be crucial for developing effective policies and support systems that promote the successful integration and economic contribution of immigrant entrepreneurs. By focusing on the unique challenges and opportunities faced by different immigrant groups, policymakers can create a more inclusive and supportive environment for all entrepreneurs in Sweden.

References

Abebe, S. A. (2019). Taking stock and moving forward in research on refugee entrepreneurship: A systematic review of the current field and future research direction. In V. Ratten & L. Dana (Eds.), *Diversity and entrepreneurship* (pp. 23–62). Routledge.

Abebe, S. A. (2023). Refugee entrepreneurship: Systematic and thematic analyses and a research agenda. *Small Business Economics, 60*(1), 315–350.

Akhtar, R. (2024). *What if your world is outside the oyster? How highly educated and skilled first-generation immigrant entrepreneurs develop opportunities in knowledge-intensive sectors.* PhD Theses. Department of Business Administration, Stockholm University.

Aldén, L., & Hammarstedt, M. (2015). *Utrikes födda på den svenska arbetsmarknaden—En översikt och en internationell jämförelse, Arbetsmarknadsreformer för jobb och välfärd.* Rapport från Socialdemokraternas forskningskommission.

Amin, S. (2002). Om kapitalismens kris och "den kulturella mångfalden". In M. Dahlberg & I. Lindberg (Eds.), *Det slutna folkhemmet: Om etniska klyftor och blågul självbild* (pp. 204–219). Agora.

Andersson, R. (2002). Boendesegregation och etniska hierarkier. In M. Dahlberg & I. Lindberg (Eds.), *Det slutna folkhemmet: Om etniska klyftor och blågul självbild* (pp. 94–115). Agora.

Andersson, L., & Hammarstedt, M. (2015). Ethnic enclaves, networks and self-employment among Middle Eastern immigrants in Sweden. *International Migration, 53*(6), 27–40.

Andersson Joona, P. (2019). *Integrationspolitiska insatser för nyanlända. Vilken roll spelar egenföretagande?* Entreprenörskapsforum.

Andersson, M., & Larsson, J. P. (2016). Local entrepreneurship clusters in cities. *Journal of Economic Geography, 16*(1), 39–66.

Andersson, M., Larsson, J. P., & Öner, Ö. (2021). Ethnic enclaves and self-employment among Middle Eastern immigrants in Sweden: Ethnic capital or enclave size? *Regional Studies, 55*(4), 590–604.

Aronsson, R. (1991). *Self-employment: A labor market perspective.* ILR Press.

Åslund, O., Erikson, R., Nordström Skans, O., & Sjögren, A. (2006). *Fritt inträde? Ungdomars och invandrares väg till det första arbetet.* SNS förlag.

Backman, M., & Karlsson, C. (2024). Ageing places: Convergence and the role of the foreign population. *Regional Studies, 58*(5), 922–937.
Backman, M., Lopez, E., & Rowe, F. (2021). The occupational trajectories and outcomes of forced migrants in Sweden. Entrepreneurship, employment or persistent inactivity? *Small Business Economics, 56*(3), 963–983.
Bansak, C., Simpson, N., & Zavodny, M. (2021). *The economics of immigration.* Routledge.
Behre, G., Larsson, L. O., & Österberg, E. (1985). *Sveriges historia 1521–1809.* Esselte Studium.
Berend, I. T., & Ranki, G. (1982). *The European periphery and industrialization 1780–1914.* Akadémiai Kiadó.
Bevelander, P. (2011). The employment integration of resettled refugees, asylum claimants and family reunion migrants in Sweden. *Refugee Survey Quarterly, 30*(1), 22–43.
Broomé, P., Bäcklund, A. K., Lundh, C., & Ohlsson, R. (1998). *Varför sitter 'brassen' på bänken? Eller varför har invandrarna så svårt att få jobb?* SNS förlag.
Bunar, N. (2002). De andra(s) skolor(na)—Från pedagogisk experimentverkstad till socialt problem? In M. Dahlberg & I. Lindberg (Eds.), *Det slutna folkhemmet: Om etniska klyftor och blågul självbild* (pp. 136–151). Agora.
Carlson, B., & Schölin, T. (2016). *Etnisk företagande som startmotor.* Timbro.
Catomeris, C. (2002). Det svartvita tänkandet. In M. Dahlberg & I. Lindberg (Eds.), *Det slutna folkhemmet: Om etniska klyftor och blågul självbild* (pp. 62–77). Agora.
Dahlstedt, M. (2002). Den mångfaldiga representationen—Det monokulturella partilivet i kritisk belysning. In M. Dahlberg & I. Lindberg (Eds.), *Det slutna folkhemmet: Om etniska klyftor och blågul självbild* (pp. 152–171). Agora.
Dahlström, C. (2004). *Nästan välkomna. Invandrarpolitikens retorik och praktik.* Doktorsavhandling, Statsvetenskapliga institutionen, Göteborgs universitet.
de los Reyes, P. (2002). Den svenska jämställdhetens etniska gränser—Om patriarkala enklaver och kulturella frizoner. In M. Dahlberg & I. Lindberg (Eds.), *Det slutna folkhemmet: Om etniska klyftor och blågul självbild* (pp. 172–187). Agora.
Diaz Ruiz, C., & Nilsson, T. (2022). Disinformation and echo chambers: How disinformation circulates on social media through identity-driven controversies. *Journal of Public Policy & Marketing, 42*(1), 18–35.
Edin, P. A., Fredriksson, P., & Åslund, O. (2003). Ethnic enclaves and the economic success of immigrants—Evidence from a natural experiment. *Quarterly Journal of Economics, 118*(1), 329–357.
Eklund, J. E., & Larsson, J. P. (2023). *Det nya utanförskapet.* Ekerlids förlag.
Embiricos, A. (2020). From refugee to entrepreneur? Challenges to refugee self-reliance in Berlin, Germany. *Journal of Refugee Studies, 33*(1), 245–267.

Eriksson, B., & Larsson, P. (2001). *Starta eget-bidrag—En studie av framgångar och misslyckanden*. IFAU forskningsrapport 2001:8.

Evansluong, Q. (2016). *Opportunity creation as a mixed embedding process: A study of immigrant entrepreneurs in Sweden*. PhD thesis, Jönköping International Business School.

Evansluong, Q., Ramirez Pasillas, M., & Nguyen Bergström, H. (2019). From breaking-ice to breaking-out: Integration as an opportunity creation process. *International Journal of Entrepreneurial Behaviour and Research, 25*(5), 880–899.

Gustafsson, B., Zamanian-B, M., & Aguilar, R. (1990). *Invandring och försörjning*. Daidalos.

Gustafsson, B., Mac Innes, H., & Österberg, T. (2017). Age at immigration matters for labor market integration—The Swedish example. *IZA Journal of Migration, 7*, 1. https://doi.org/10.1186/s40176-016-0078-7

Häll, L. (1997). Invandrarnas levnadsförhållanden. In J. Vogel & L. Häll (Eds.), *Välfärd och ojämlikhet i 20-årsperspektiv 1975–1995* (Levnadsförhållanden Rapport 91) (pp. 467–490). Statistics Sweden.

Hammarstedt, M. (2006). The predicted earnings differential and immigrant self-employment in Sweden. *Applied Economics, 38*(6), 619–630.

Hårsman, B. (2006). Ethnic diversity and spatial segregation in the Stockholm region. *Urban Studies, 43*(8), 1341–1364.

Hartman, A. (2015). *A war for the soul of America: A history of the culture wars*. University of Chicago Press.

Heckscher, E. F. (1936). *Sveriges ekonomiska historia* (Vol. I:2). Bonniers.

Heckscher, E. F. (1949). *Sveriges ekonomiska historia* (Vol. II:1). Bonniers.

Heinö Johansson, A. (2021). *Anteckningar från kulturkriget*. Timbro.

Henreksson, M., & Stenkula, M. (2007). *Entreprenörskap på riktigt*. SNS förlag.

Hout, M., & Rosen, H. S. (1999). *Self-employment, family background and race*. National Bureau of Economic Research, NBER Working Paper 7344.

Kazlou, A. (2019). *Immigrant entrepreneurs in a changing institutional context: A mixed embeddedness approach*. PhD thesis, Linköping University Press.

Kazlou, A., & Urban, S. (2023). Swedish migration policy liberalization and new immigrant entrepreneurs. *International Migration, 61*(2), 87–106.

Klinthäll, M., Slavnic, Z., Urban, S., Mitchell, C., & Schölin, T. (2016). *Invandring och företagande*. DELMI kunskapsöversikt 2016:7.

Koleva, S. P., Graham, J., Iyer, R., Ditto, P. H., & Haidt, J. (2012). Tracing the threads: How five moral concerns (especially Purity) help explain culture war attitudes. *Journal of Research in Personality, 46*(2), 184–194.

Kordel, S., & Weidinger, T. (2018). Current processes of immigration to European peripheries: Status quo, implications and development strategies. In S. Kordel, T. Weidinger, & I. Jelen (Eds.), *Processes of immigration to European peripheries: Status quo, implications and development strategies* (pp. xv–xxx). Cambridge Scholars Publishing.

Lindgren, H. (2022). Integrationsutredningen som försvann. *Kvartal*. Retrieved June 12, 2024, from https://kvartal.se/artiklar/integrationsutredningen-revisited/

Lindkvist, T., & Ågren, K. (1985). *Sveriges medeltid*. Norstedts.

Lundh, C., & Ohlsson, R. (1994). *Från arbetskraftsimport till flyktinginvandring*. SNS förlag.

Lundh, C., Bennich-Björkman, L., Ohlsson, R., Pedersen, P. J., & Rooth, D. O. (2002). *Arbete? Var god dröj! Invandrare i välfärdssamhället*. SNS förlag.

Magnusson, L. (1999). *Merkantilism. Ett ekonomiskt tänkande formuleras*. SNS förlag.

Mattsson, K., & Tesfahuney, I. (2002). Rasism i vardagen. In M. Dahlberg & I. Lindberg (Eds.), *Det slutna folkhemmet: Om etniska klyftor och blågul självbild* (pp. 28–41). Agora.

Mitze, T., Dall Schmidt, T., Rauhut, D., & Kangasharju, A. (2018). Ageing shocks and short-run regional labour market dynamics in a spatial panel VAR approach. *Applied Economics, 50*(8), 870–890.

Molina, I. (1997). *Stadens rasifiering. Etnisk boendesegregation i folkhemmet*. Doktorsavhandling. Uppsala universitet, Institutionen för social och ekonomisk geografi.

Mulinari, D. (2002). "Det är inte rasism…"—Om facket och invandrarna. In M. Dahlberg & I. Lindberg (Eds.), *Det slutna folkhemmet: Om etniska klyftor och blågul självbild* (pp. 42–60). Agora.

Neergaard, A. (2002). Arbetsmarknadens mönster—Om rasifierad segmentering. In M. Dahlberg & I. Lindberg (Eds.), *Det slutna folkhemmet: Om etniska klyftor och blågul självbild* (pp. 116–134). Agora.

Nordlund, S. (1989). *Upptäckten av Sverige. Utländska direktinvesteringar i Sverige 1895–1945*. Umeå Studies in Economic History no. 12. Department of Economic History, Umeå University.

Nordlund, S. (1999a). Invandrarföretagande i Sverige—En historisk tillbakablick. In Kulturdepartementet, *Invandrare som företagare*, SOU 1999:49 (pp. 354–364). Regeringskansliet.

Nordlund, S. (1999b). Kommentarer eller synpunkter rörande insatser för att åstadkomma lika behandling av rörelseidkare oavsett etnisk och kulturell bakgrund. In Kulturdepartementet, *Invandrare som företagare*, SOU 1999:49 (pp. 346–353). Regeringskansliet.

Nordström Skans, O., & Åslund, O. (2009). *Segregationen i storstäderna*. SNS förlag.

NUTEK. (2001). *Marginalisering eller integration—Invandrares företagande i svensk retorik och praktik*. Nutek.

OECD (2019). Ready to help? Improving resilience of integration systems for refugees and other vulnerable migrants. .

Ohlsson, R. (1978). *Ekonomisk strukturomvandling och invandring*. CWK Gleerup.

Ohlsson, H., Broomé, P., & Bevelander, P. (2012). Self-employment of immigrants and natives in Sweden—A multilevel analysis. *Entrepreneurship and Regional Development, 24*(5–6), 405–423.

Popoola, M. (2002). *Integration, en samtidsspegling*. Svenska kommunförbundet.

Rauhut, D. (2004). *Replacement migration to Sweden. An overview of possible sender countries*. ITPS report A2004:016, Östersund and Stockholm.

Rauhut, D. (2014). *I moder Sveas ömma famn*. Carlsons bokförlag.

Rauhut, D., & Rauhut Kompaniets, O. (2018). The impact of immigrant entrepreneurship regional development in Western Sweden. *Romanian Journal of Regional Science, 12*(1), 18–42.

Rauhut, D., Torsein, E., Widman, T., & Olsson, A. K. (2014). *Integration, entreprenörskap och hållbar samhällsutveckling*. Högskolan Väst.

Rauhut, D., Aigner-Walder, B., & Schomaker, R. (2023). *The economics of immigration beyond the cities: Theoretical perspectives and empirical insights*. Palgrave Macmillan.

Rider, C. I., Thompson, P., Kacperczyk, A., & Tåg, J. (2013). *Experience and entrepreneurship*. Research Institute of Industrial Economics, IFN Working paper No. 970.

Ruist, J. (2015). The fiscal cost of refugee immigration: The example of Sweden. *Population and Development Review, 41*(4), 567–581.

SCB. (2015). *Vuxna med svaga färdigheter*. Temarapport 2015:2 Utbildning. Statistiska Centralbyrån.

SCB. (2024). *PIAAC—Den internationella undersökningen av vuxnas färdigheter*. Retrieved January 28, 2025, from https://www.scb.se/contentassets/43fec92b83c24a60aebb22150d6d59fa/uf0546_2022a01_br_a40br2404.pdf

Skaug, J. E. (2000). *En förstudie om entreprenörskap: En kartläggning av tidigare forskning och utredningar om entreprenörskap, entreprenöriellt arbete och ledarskap*. Institutionen för arbete, ekonomi och hälsa, Högskolan Trollhättan/Uddevalla.

Slavnik, Z. (2013). Immigrant small business in Sweden: A critical review of the development of a research field. *Journal of Business Administration Research, 2*(1), 29–42.

Svanberg, I., & Tydén, M. (1992). *Tusen år av invandring*. Gidlunds bokförlag.

Tavassoli, S., & Trippl, M. (2019). The impact of ethnic communities on immigrant entrepreneurship: Evidence from Sweden. *Regional Studies, 53*(1), 67–79.

Tempsch, R. (1997). *Från Centraleuropa till Folkhemmet: den sudet-tyska invandringen till Sverige 1938–1955*. Meddelanden från Ekonomisk-historiska institutionen vid Göteborgs universitet, nr. 73.

Tillväxtverket. (2017). *Starta företag i Sverige*. Retrieved April 12, 2024, from https://tillvaxtverket.se/download/18.6855bfcf184896002ffa1f/1668765691293/Starta%20fo%CC%88retag%20i%20Sverige%20-%20svenska.pdf

Verksamt. (2024). *Starta företag som asylsökande eller nyanländ*. Retrieved April 12, 2024, from https://verksamt.se/starta-foretag/starta-foretag-som-utlandsk-medborgare/starta-foretag-som-asylsokande-eller-nyanland

Wennberg, K., & Efendic, N. (2013). *Bakgrund och framgång—Vad avgör om företag växer?* FORES Studie 2013:2.

Widmalm, S. (2019). De integrationspolitiska utredningarna som kulturkrig. *Respons, 2019*(6), 19–25.

Zalkat, G. (2024). *Immigrant entrepreneurship in Sweden: Challenges and opportunities related to business development*. PhD Thesis. Halmstad University Press.

CHAPTER 6

Policy Aspects

Abstract This chapter provides an overview on what support forms exist to stimulate immigrant entrepreneurship and how efficient these policies are will also be discussed. How to define immigrant entrepreneurs is crucial when discussing policy aspects related to immigrant entrepreneurship.

Keywords Legal framework • Support mechanisms • Capital access • Policy effectiveness • Institutional change

When politicians want to change something so that development goes in a socially desirable direction, efforts can be made in different ways. Policy initiatives to facilitate or hinder entrepreneurship are an opportunity. The business freedom ordinance of 1864 is a telling example of how the state tried to prevent immigrant entrepreneurship. Today, the political rhetoric is more about what policy efforts are being made and should be made to stimulate immigrant entrepreneurship in Sweden. The discussion begins by describing how and who can start a business in Sweden, followed by what forms of support are available. The discussion then focuses on what and how these contemporary support forms actually support immigrant entrepreneurship.

D. Rauhut, *Immigrant Entrepreneurship in Sweden*,
https://doi.org/10.1007/978-3-032-02466-4_6

The question of what support foreign entrepreneurs seeking to relocate to Sweden historically enjoyed is intriguing. Knowledge in this area is, to say the least, very fragmented. Apart from letters of privilege from the King, tax breaks, and monopolistic concessions, few other forms of support appear to have been implemented during the Middle Ages to attract foreign entrepreneurs to Sweden (Nordlund, 1999). During the mercantilist era, many foreign entrepreneurs starting their businesses in Sweden benefitted from government subsidies (Magnusson, 1987) and monopolistic concessions (Nordlund, 1999). When Sweden commenced the industrialisation process, the country adhered to a classical liberal path with limited public financial support to private companies; however, the State invested heavily in infrastructure (Berend & Ranki, 1982). Furthermore, the Swedish state enacted laws against foreign entrepreneurs and regulated their businesses (Nordlund, 1999).

6.1 Contemporary Legal Framework for Company Startups

To start a limited company in Sweden, one must be at least 18 years old. However, individuals aged 16 can start a trading company or sole proprietorship with guardian permission (Skatteverket, 2024). EU/EEA citizens can live and work in any EU country, including Sweden, without a residence permit if they can support themselves. Non-EU/EEA citizens planning to stay in Sweden for more than three months to run a business must obtain a residence permit before entering Sweden. The Tax Agency assigns a coordination number for VAT registration (Verksamt, 2024). This number is for individuals who need to be registered but are not eligible for a regular Swedish personal identity number. For non-EU/EEA citizens, the Migration Agency assesses the applicant's business plans for a residence permit. Applicants must show they can support themselves and have sufficient capital to run the business for at least two years. Income from multiple jobs and the business can be combined (Tillväxtverket, 2017).

Both asylum seekers and newly arrived individuals can start a business in Sweden. Asylum seekers can start a business upon submitting their application, while new arrivals can start a company under the same terms as Swedish citizens. A newly arrived person is someone who has just received a residence permit (Verksamt, 2024). Asylum seekers who start a business cannot change visa categories if their asylum application is rejected. However, those employed for four months with a promise of continued employment for at least 12 months can apply for a work permit or start a company after a rejection (Tillväxtverket, 2017).

6.2 Support for Entrepreneurs

The few studies that exist conclude that it is important that efforts to support immigrant entrepreneurship do not replace measures for labour market integration. Many initiatives have aimed to promote entrepreneurship as an alternative to unemployment for the foreign-born, which often results in people who become self-employed becoming stuck in small-scale, less profitable business (Klinthäll et al., 2016). Well-educated immigrants with good business plans and an entrepreneurial mindset perform well in Sweden. Running a business in contexts with people belonging to the same country of origin limits growth potential (Akhtar, 2024).

There are several forms of support for entrepreneurs who want to start a company. Unemployed individuals considering starting a business can receive support from the *Public Employment Service* (PES), known as 'support for starting a business'. This grant helps guarantee a livelihood during the initial phase of the business. The PES decides eligibility based on the potential profitability and long-term viability of the business. The allowance is paid for up to six months and matches what the individual would receive in unemployment compensation (Arbetsföremedlingen, 2024).

Nyföretagarcentrum (in English: Centre for New Entrepreneurs), established in 1985 to counter industrial closures and stimulate economic development, has expanded to over 200 municipalities. Today, every tenth company in Sweden is started through Nyföretagarcentrum, with over 250,000 companies launched to date. About 37 percent of these companies are run by immigrants. The main support includes advice, education on starting and developing a company, business plans, mentorship, and networking opportunities (NyföretagarCentrum, 2024).

Companies across the country can apply for regional business support, such as consulting assistance or investments, from the relevant region or county board. Some grants are specific to certain geographic areas or industries (Företagarna, 2024). These include:

- *Investment grants*: For smaller investments like new machines or premises.
- *Consultant checks*: To hire external consultants.
- *Collaboration projects*: For joint projects between multiple companies.

- *Micro-support, innovation support, or loans*: For businesses in nature tourism, innovative sectors, or research investments.
- *Transport grants*: For industries in northern Sweden processing products in the four northernmost counties.
- *Larger investment grants*: Available for companies in Norrland or northwestern Svealand.

Other actors also offer financial support to newly started companies:

- *VINNOVA*: The government agency promoting innovation provides grants for innovation projects and research. Smaller supports like planning and operating grants are also available (VINNOVA, 2021).
- *Swedish Board of Agriculture*: Offers special support for startups in the agricultural sector, including farmer support, business and project support, and market support (Jordbruksverket, 2024).
- *Enterprise Europe Network*: Assists small- and medium-sized companies with information and advice on EU rules and funding, and mediates business contacts (Enterprise Europe Network, 2024).
- *EU SME Support*: Helps small- and medium-sized companies apply for EU funding (EU SME Support, 2024).
- *IFS*: A charity foundation supporting immigrant entrepreneurship in Sweden since 1996. IFS helps entrepreneurs with a foreign background to start, run, and develop businesses. They provide support in starting and developing businesses, coaching, mentoring, networking, and project management. IFS operates in 15 locations with 32 employees offering advice in 28 languages (IFS, 2024).[1]

Worth noting is that these potential funders do not target investments in low-productive and labour-intensive business such as e.g., convenience stores, pizzerias, taxis, or industrial cleaning companies. Their target group is different: companies that can grow fast, expand, and generate profit on the invested money. These companies are usually characterised

[1] In 2007, IFS became part of ALMI. ALMI, which is owned by the state together with regional owners, consists of the parent company and 21 regional subsidiaries. ALMI's mission is to create growth and renewal in the business world through financing in combination with business development. The goal is that more innovative ideas are successfully commercialised, that more viable companies are started and developed, and that more companies increase their competitiveness and growth (ALMI, 2007).

by being high-productive and capital-intensive. Those who wants to start a company which is low-productive and labour-intensive must find financial support elsewhere.

6.3 Challenges for Support and Funding

The potential support from different providers entails several conditions that entrepreneurs must meet. The minimum requirements include having a well-thought-out business plan, the potential to generate profit over time, and financial viability (Arbetsföremedlingen, 2024). If an entrepreneur has an innovative idea that receives financial support, investors often want a say in the company's development, which can reduce the entrepreneur's control. If the entrepreneur is not eligible for support or wishes to maintain full control, alternative financing must be sought. This poses a significant challenge to many immigrant entrepreneurs.

Limited access to financial capital is a significant obstacle for entrepreneurship among certain immigrant groups. However, the knowledge of the immigrants' entrepreneurial financing is fragmented and under-researched. Malki et al. (2020) note in their systematic literature review that international research point at informal financing as preferred by immigrant entrepreneurs, and that perceived forms of different types of discrimination hinder them from financing their businesses. Self-employed non-European immigrants report more discrimination by banks compared to natives and European immigrants. Immigrant-owned firms apply for bank loans more frequently than native-owned firms but face higher denial rates and interest rates (Aldén & Hammarstedt, 2016). Research in the USA has also identified ethnic discrimination in the bank loan market (Asiedu et al., 2012; Blanchard et al., 2008).

Securing funding for a business venture poses significant challenges for many immigrant entrepreneurs. It is essential for financial institutions to recognise that numerous immigrant entrepreneurs face religious constraints, such as restrictions on paying interest rates. Consequently, specialised financial arrangements tailored to these entrepreneurs are necessary (Malki, 2024). In the absence of such provisions, family networks appear to play a crucial role in mitigating resource shortages for refugee entrepreneurs, enabling these businesses to establish themselves and sustain operations over extended periods (Kazlou, 2019).

The reasons why immigrant entrepreneurs struggle to secure financing are seldom explored beyond the issue of discrimination. Non-European immigrants are overrepresented in low-productivity, labour-intensive industries like wholesale, retail, auto repair, removal services, taxis, cafés, and pizzerias, which often struggle with profitability and financial viability (Rauhut & Rauhut Kompaniets, 2018). To be eligible for financial startup support, a company must have a well-developed business plan, the potential for long-term profitability, and financial viability. Insufficiently detailed business plans may also contribute to higher interest rates as lenders compensate for higher risks. Alternatively, lenders may reject entrepreneurs and refuse to provide financing.

Efendic et al. (2015) identify key factors related to immigrant entrepreneurship in their study. Their findings reveal that firms established by second-generation immigrants from OECD countries demonstrate higher growth rates than those owned by native entrepreneurs, whereas the opposite is observed among second-generation immigrants from non-OECD countries. This suggests that economic integration, in terms of small business growth among immigrants in Sweden, is characterised by segmented rather than universal assimilation.

The divergence in entrepreneurial development between second-generation immigrants from OECD and non-OECD countries can largely be attributed to sectoral differences in business establishment. Specifically, second-generation non-OECD immigrants, along with first-generation immigrants, are more likely to establish businesses within low-productivity, labour-intensive industries compared to natives and second-generation OECD immigrants (Efendic et al., 2015). Given the inherently slim profit margins in such industries, launching and sustaining businesses in these sectors presents considerable challenges, necessitating a well-structured and carefully considered business plan to secure financing.

The challenges faced by entrepreneurs are similar regardless of whether they are native-born or immigrants. Essential prerequisites include the existence of a market for the product or service, a well-developed business plan, and sufficient startup capital. Additionally, the rules, laws, and regulations apply equally to both native and immigrant entrepreneurs. There is no preferential treatment for native entrepreneurs, nor are immigrant entrepreneurs disadvantaged due to their background or nationality (Justitiedepartementet, 2003).

6.4 What Policies?

The National Audit Office has examined whether the Swedish parliament's prioritisation of women and people with a foreign background have had an impact on the state's business promotion efforts. The review has included the government, Nutek,[2] the state-owned company ALMI Företagspartner AB with its 21 regional subsidiaries, and the Public Employment Service in terms of the support for starting a business (the so-called startup grant). Women and people with a foreign background are seen as a partially untapped potential to create more and growing companies. Several studies have also shown that these groups face particular obstacles in their entrepreneurship, e.g. when applying for a loan. The review shows that the prioritisation of women and people with a foreign background had little impact. The target groups are not clearly defined, which above all applies to the group of people with a foreign background. The National Audit Office also states that the integration policy assumes that people and groups should not be singled out based on their origin. Interventions must instead be adapted based on the needs of different individuals (Riksrevisionen, 2007). If the interventions are based on the needs of the single individual, it means in practical terms that the individual business plan for each of the credit applications is at the centre of the decision to grant a loan or not. Already Gustafsson et al. (1990) concluded that the immigrant entrepreneurs operate in business with lower profitability than natives, which makes it more difficult for them to obtain loans to start up the business. A similar conclusion was made by Klinthäll et al. (2016). Consequently, it cannot be ruled out that some of the applications for loans may not be denied because the applicant is an immigrant, but because the company has meagre prospects of being profitable. Although such argument and reasoning appear logical, the Swedish scholarship on immigrant entrepreneurship leans towards the discrimination discourse (see e.g., Aldén & Hammarstedt, 2016; Klinthäll et al., 2016; Zalkat, 2024; Bursell, 2014; Erlandsson, 2024).

There are more ways to stimulate immigrant entrepreneurship than facilitating financing and loan credits. The public sector can also, at least in theory, stimulate immigrant entrepreneurship during procurement. While EU procurement rules allow that social considerations can be taken into account in procurement, Swedish legislation opposes this. According to

[2] Today the same authority is called Tillväxtverket.

the Swedish procurement rules, only financial and business considerations can be considered in public procurement. As EU law is above the Swedish legislation, it is not self-evident whether the Swedish legislation takes precedence in the interpretation of the rules (Rauhut & Alander, 2007).

6.5 Summary

The legal framework for starting a business in Sweden requires meeting age and residency criteria. EU/EEA citizens can work without a permit, while non-EU/EEA citizens need a residence permit and sufficient capital. Asylum seekers can start businesses but face restrictions if their applications are rejected. Support for entrepreneurs includes grants, mentorship, and networking from organisations like Nyföretagarcentrum and VINNOVA, targeting high-productive, capital-intensive ventures. However, low-productive, labour-intensive businesses must find alternative funding.

Despite targeted support policies, the National Audit Office found limited impact on women and people with foreign backgrounds due to unclear target group definitions and a focus on individual needs rather than group origin. This approach led to difficulties for immigrant entrepreneurs, who often operate in less profitable sectors, making it harder to secure loans. Public procurement could stimulate immigrant entrepreneurship, but Swedish legislation limits this to financial considerations.

A significant issue is defining immigrant entrepreneurship. Ownership and control are crucial, with sole proprietorships and partnerships easier to classify. The 1995 EU membership shifted the definition of immigrant entrepreneurs, highlighting the need for further research on these institutional changes. Refugee entrepreneurship remains under-researched, with distinct challenges compared to other immigrants. Sweden offers special visas for non-EU entrepreneurs, though most are granted to individuals from the Middle East and Africa starting businesses in low-skilled service sectors.

References

Akhtar, R. (2024). *What if your world is outside the oyster? How highly educated and skilled first-generation immigrant entrepreneurs develop opportunities in knowledge-intensive sectors*. PhD Theses. Department of Business Administration, Stockholm University.

Aldén, L., & Hammarstedt, M. (2016). Discrimination in the credit market? Access to financial capital among self-employed immigrants. *Kyklos, 69*(1), 3–31.

ALMI. (2007). *IFS integreras med Almi—En historisk händelse.* Pressmeddelande 2007-05-30. Retrieved April 15, 2024, from https://press.almi.se/posts/pressreleases/ifs-integreras-med-almi%2D%2D-en-historisk-handel

Arbetsföremedlingen. (2024). *Starta eget, stöd till start av näringsverksamhet.* Retrieved April 12, 2024, from https://arbetsformedlingen.se/for-arbetssokande/extra-stod/stod-a-o/starta-eget-stod-till-start-av-naringsverksamhet

Asiedu, E., Freeman, J. A., & Nti-Addae, A. (2012). Access to credit by small businesses: How relevant are race, ethnicity, and gender? *American Economic Review, 102*(3), 532–537.

Berend, I. T., & Ranki, G. (1982). *The European periphery and industrialization 1780–1914.* Akadémiai Kiadó.

Blanchard, L., Zhao, B., & Yinger, J. (2008). Do lenders discriminate against minority and woman entrepreneurs? *Journal of Urban Economics, 63*, 467–497.

Bursell, M. (2014). The multiple burdens of foreign-named men: Evidence from a field experiment on gendered ethnic hiring discrimination in Sweden. *European Sociological Review, 30*(3), 399–409.

Efendic, N., Andersson, F. W., & Wennberg, K. (2015). Growth in first- and second-generation immigrant firms in Sweden. *International Small Business Journal, 34*(8), 1028–1052.

Enterprise Europe Network. (2024). *Homepage.* Retrieved April 17, 2024, from https://een.ec.europa.eu/

Erlandsson, A. (2024). Gendered ethnic discrimination and the role of recruiter gender. A field experiment. *Acta Sociologica, 67*(2), 232–250.

EU SME Support. (2024). *Villkor för EU-finansiering till små och medelstora företag.* Retrieved April 17, 2024, from https://eusme.se/jag-vill-veta-mer-om-eu-finansiering/

Företagarna. (2024). *Starta eget bidrag.* Retrieved April 12, 2024, from https://www.foretagarna.se/driva-eget-foretag/starta-eget-foretag/starta-eget-bidrag/

Gustafsson, B., Zamanian-B, M., & Aguilar, R. (1990). *Invandring och försörjning.* Daidalos.

IFS. (2024). *LinkedIn page.* Retrieved April 15, 2024.

Jordbruksverket. (2024). *Stöd till lantbrukare och verksamma på landsbygden.* Retrieved April 15, 2024, from https://jordbruksverket.se/stod

Justitiedepartementet. (2003). *Diskrimineras invandrarföretagare i Sverige? En empirisk studie av småföretagskonkurser under 1990-talet.* Rapport från Integrationspolitiska maktutredningen SOU2003:17. Fritzes.

Kazlou, A. (2019). *Immigrant entrepreneurs in a changing institutional context: A mixed embeddedness approach.* PhD thesis, Linköping University Press.

Klinthäll, M., Slavnic, Z., Urban, S., Mitchell, C., & Schölin, T. (2016). *Invandring och företagande*. DELMI kunskapsöversikt 2016:7.

Magnusson, L. (1987). Mercantilism and "reform" mercantilism: The rise of economic discourse in Sweden during the eighteenth century. *History of Political Economy, 19*(3), 415–433.

Malki, B. (2024). Responding to financing uncertainty in complex settings: The case of immigrant entrepreneurs from the Arab world in Sweden. *Entrepreneurship & Regional Development, 36*(3–4), 366–385.

Malki, B., Uman, T., & Pittino, D. (2020). The entrepreneurial financing of the immigrant entrepreneurs: A literature review. *Small Business Economics, 58*(3), 1337–1365.

Nordlund, S. (1999). Invandrarföretagande i Sverige—En historisk tillbakablick. In Kulturdepartementet, Invandrare som företagare, SOU 1999:49 (pp. 354–364). Regeringskansliet.

Nyföretagarcentrum. (2024). *Historik/bakgrund*. Retrieved April 15, 2024, from https://www.nyforetagarcentrum.com/nyforetagarcentrum-sverige/historikbakgrund/

Rauhut, D., & Alander, N. (2007). Invandrarföretagande och integration. Om främjande kommunala insatser. In D. Rauhut (Ed.), *Vägen till Sverige—Om Stockholms stads integrationsarbete*. FoU-rapport 2007:1 (pp. 97–103). Stadsledningskontoret, Stockholms stad.

Rauhut, D., & Rauhut Kompaniets, O. (2018). The impact of immigrant entrepreneurship regional development in Western Sweden. *Romanian Journal of Regional Science, 12*(1), 18–42.

Riksrevisionen. (2007). *Statens företagsfrämjande insatser. Når de kvinnor och personer med utländsk bakgrund?* RiR rapport 2007:11.

Skatteverket. (2024). *Starta och registrera företag*. Retrieved April 12, 2024, from https://www.skatteverket.se/foretag/drivaforetag/startaochregistrera.4.58d555751259e4d661680006123.html

Tillväxtverket. (2017). *Starta företag i Sverige*. Retrieved April 12, 2024, from https://tillvaxtverket.se/download/18.6855bfcf184896002ffa1f/1668765691293/Starta%20fo%CC%88retag%20i%20Sverige%20-%20svenska.pdf

Verksamt. (2024). *Starta företag som asylsökande eller nyanländ*. Retrieved April 12, 2024, from https://verksamt.se/starta-foretag/starta-foretag-som-utlandsk-medborgare/starta-foretag-som-asylsokande-eller-nyanland

VINNOVA. (2021). *Regler och villkor för finansiering*. Retrieved April 15, 2024, from https://www.vinnova.se/sok-finansiering/regler-for-finansiering/

Zalkat, G. (2024). *Immigrant entrepreneurship in Sweden: Challenges and opportunities related to business development*. PhD Thesis. Halmstad University Press.

CHAPTER 7

Comparative Perspectives

Abstract This chapter discusses immigrant entrepreneurship in Sweden from a comparative perspective. The general trends and development in immigrant entrepreneurship in some European are presented as well as contemporary policy incentives in these countries to enhance immigrant entrepreneurship. Moreover, to what extent the development in immigrant entrepreneurship can represent a Swedish 'Sonderweg' or not is also discussed.

Keywords Sonderweg • Comparative trends • Urban concentration • Low-productivity sectors • Policy landscape

7.1 Introduction

This chapter provides a comprehensive examination of immigrant entrepreneurship in Sweden from a comparative perspective. It discusses contemporary trends observed in other European countries, exploring how these trends align or contrast with those in Sweden. By examining the various policy approaches across Europe, the chapter aims to shed light on the strategies that different countries employ to support and integrate immigrant entrepreneurs into their economies. By situating Sweden within the wider European context, the chapter provides a nuanced

D. Rauhut, *Immigrant Entrepreneurship in Sweden*,
https://doi.org/10.1007/978-3-032-02466-4_7

understanding of how different countries navigate the complexities of supporting immigrant entrepreneurs.

The discussion begins with an overview of the current landscape of immigrant entrepreneurship, highlighting the sectors in which immigrants are predominantly active and the geographical distribution of their businesses. The chapter then transitions to a discussion of policy frameworks, assessing how initiatives and regulations in countries like e.g., the UK, Germany, and Italy influence the entrepreneurial activities of immigrants.

One of the key themes explored in this chapter is the concept of a Swedish 'Sonderweg'—a unique path in the development of immigrant entrepreneurship. By comparing Sweden's approach to those of other nations, the chapter investigates whether Sweden's policies and practices represent a distinct model. This includes examining the integration of refugees into the entrepreneurial ecosystem, the role of social welfare systems, and the challenges faced by immigrant entrepreneurs in Sweden.

7.2 Contemporary Trends in Other Countries

In Austria, immigrant entrepreneurship is dominating a few sectors and industries. Immigrant entrepreneurs hold a significant share of the entrepreneurs operating in the construction sector, industrial cleaning, care taking sector, transport and restaurants. The common denominator is that these sectors are low-productive and labour-intensive. While almost 50 percent of all immigrant entrepreneurs in Austria are in the City of Vienna, only 7 percent are in Carinthia (Gruber & Rauhut, 2024). Most immigrant entrepreneurship in Bulgaria is found in low-productive and labour-intensive industries such as e.g., hairdressers, cafés, retail etc. Not much startup capital is needed, and it is possible to make a living on the company (Krasteva, 2021).

A majority of those migrating to Finland do so because of family ties. The second largest immigrant group is not 'immigrants' in a legal sense—they are EU citizens and hence not immigrants. The EU citizens have come to Finland for studies or jobs. Immigrant entrepreneurs are mainly found among refugees. Restaurants, cleaning services and grocery stores are common immigrant businesses, and they are usually started to escape unemployment (Davydova-Minguet et al., 2021). The immigrant entrepreneurs are not innovative, but they are good at market and product development. One such example is to introduce home delivery of food in rural parts of Finland (Rauhut et al., 2021).

Grocery stores, cafés, restaurants, and care services are common sectors of immigrant entrepreneurship in Germany. Most immigrant entrepreneurship target the own immigrant community with demanded goods and services. The bigger the city, the bigger demand for these services, and vice versa, which means that most immigrant entrepreneurship is found in the cities. The introduction of new services and products by immigrants are, however, mistaken for being 'innovative'. Introducing new products and services to the local economy, such as kebabs, pizzas, Southeast Asian cuisine, and massages, can significantly boost community engagement. Being pioneers in offering new delivery methods like take-away food, or selling unique produce such as halal meat, fresh vegetables, and exotic spices, fills a gap in the market and meets previously unmet local demands (Kordel & Weidinger, 2021). However, this is not about innovations, but market and product development (Rauhut et al., 2023).

Immigrant entrepreneurs in Italy are primarily involved in services, retail, and construction. Services constitute the largest share, with many businesses focusing on retail and personal services. The clothing manufacturing sector also sees a high percentage of immigrant entrepreneurship (Dudi et al., 2021). The majority of immigrant-run companies are located in metropolitan areas, particularly in the central and northern regions of Italy. Lombardy (Milan) and Lazio (Rome) are the epicentres, with Lombardy having the highest number of immigrant-led businesses. Urban centres provide better access to resources, networks, and markets, which are crucial for business growth (Paoloni et al., 2024). From 2011 to 2022, businesses managed by migrants grew by 42.7 percent, while companies managed by Italians experienced a decline. Immigrant entrepreneurs are often sole proprietors, but there has been a rise in corporations conducted by migrants. The majority of immigrant entrepreneurs are under the age of 50, and women represent a significant and growing component of this group (Aliaga-Isla & Rialp, 2013). The Italian National Strategy for Inner Areas (SNAI) considers immigrants to play a crucial role in revitalising the country's inner regions. It views immigration as a sign of vitality, as these often-deserted areas typically consist of small communities that lack youth and innovation, and now the immigrants bring that in (Bona et al., 2021).

Most of the immigrants to Norway who startup businesses are generally not especially innovative. Generally, they start businesses such as cafés and grocery stores (Røhnebæk et al., 2021). These immigrant entrepreneurs have contributed to an expansion and diversification of products and services (Blumenthal & Lund, 2021). However, immigrant entrepreneurs experience bankruptcy to a larger extent than native entrepreneurs do, which indicates that the immigrant entrepreneurs operate in businesses and industries with narrow profit margins (Vinogradov & Isaksen, 2008; Naz, 2017).

The sector in Spain with the highest activity of immigrant entrepreneurs is the small commerce sector. These entrepreneurs generally enter the ethnical market with their service or product. Groceries, restaurants, hairdressers/barbers etc. are common activities. Immigrant entrepreneurship can be found in smaller towns and villages, but immigrants generally start their company close to the target audience—immigrants—and they are found in bigger towns and cities. Most of the companies started by immigrants are low-productive and labour-intensive, and they aim at escaping unemployment (Vitores et al., 2020; Riesco-Sanz, 2008).

Immigrants are involved in a wide range of sectors, but they are particularly prominent in technology, finance, retail, and hospitality (Levie, 2007). The majority of immigrant-founded companies are located in metropolitan areas, especially in cities like London, Birmingham, and Manchester. These cities offer a vibrant ecosystem with access to resources, networks, and markets that are crucial for business growth (Hyams-Ssekasi & Chimenya, 2024). Immigrants are overrepresented among the UK's fastest-growing startups. Just less than 40 percent of the UK's fastest-growing startups have at least one immigrant co-founder. This highlights the significant contribution of immigrant entrepreneurs to the UK's economy (Dheer, 2018). However, immigrant entrepreneurs are also overrepresented in the startups of low-productive and labour-intensive service sector jobs in the UK. This trend is similar to what has been observed in other countries, where immigrants often turn to sectors like retail, hospitality, and personal services due to barriers in accessing more capital-intensive industries (Ram & Jones, 2008; Ram et al., 2017).

Compared to the development in Sweden, three characteristics appear to be similar among the reviewed countries. One is that immigrant entrepreneurs are clustering in low-productive and labour-intensive sectors, such as e.g., restaurants, cafés, cleaning services, hairdressers and barbers, grocery stores, construction and transport services. To start a company in these sectors generally requires relatively little startup capital.

A second common characteristic is that immigrant entrepreneurship predominantly takes place in bigger cities. This is related to the fact that immigrant entrepreneurship generally targets a demand in the own immigrant community; in bigger cities there are more fellow compatriots than in smaller towns in rural and peripheral areas. Being close to the market is crucial for labour-intensive and low-productive businesses. When analysing company startups and non-EU28 population, i.e., immigrants, in NUTS2 regions without cities exceeding 250,000 inhabitants, a low but negative correlation exists (see Fig. 7.1). This means that a higher share of the non-EU28 population leads to fewer company startups. A consequence of these empirical findings for NUTS2 regions without cities exceeding 250,000 inhabitants is that the widely held notion that immigrants are more entrepreneurial than natives and that they start businesses in non-metropolitan regions can be questioned (Rauhut et al., 2023).

The third common trait pertains to innovations. Innovations involve the commercial use of new technologies, materials, methods, or energy sources. It is important to distinguish innovations from the introduction of existing products and services to either current or new markets (Flikkema et al., 2007; Rydvalova & Skala, 2021). Immigrants can play a significant role in innovation by generating unique ideas for products or processes. However, there is often confusion between innovations and market or product development. For instance, launching a restaurant,

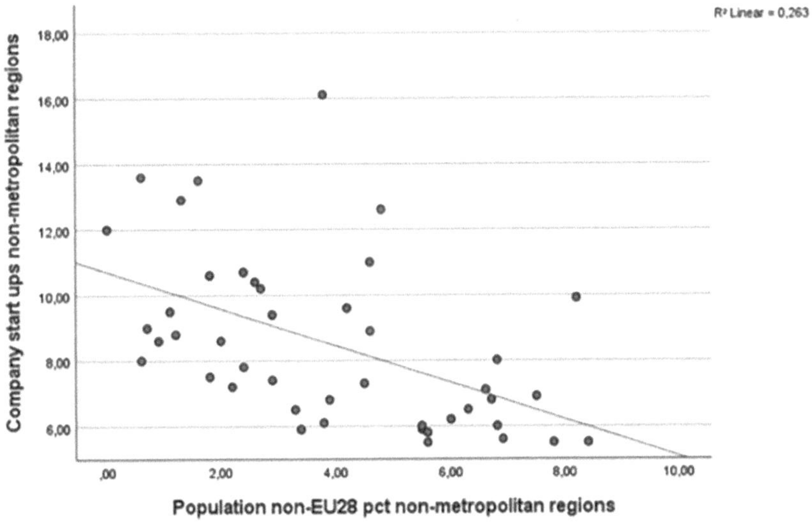

Fig. 7.1 Company startups and non-EU28 population in NUTS2 regions without cities exceeding 250,000 inhabitants (non-metropolitan regions) in 2019. Source: Rauhut et al. (2023)

take-away service, or home delivery service in a previously unserved area is about market and product development and not innovation (Kotler et al., 2020).

7.3 Policy Perspectives

The discussion in Chap. 6 puts the finger on the fact that there are very few policies that explicitly target immigrant entrepreneurship in Sweden. To what extent this is unique for Sweden is worth discussing. Hence, this section will provide an overview on what policies exist targeting immigrant entrepreneurship in other EU Member States. The current focus on immigrant entrepreneurship in Austria targets the cities, which is logical as most immigrants live in the cities. Although there is a broad offer of information and counselling provided by specialised institutions, many migrant entrepreneurs trust the advice and experiences of other migrant entrepreneurs more than official channels. One possible explanation for this may be related to the fact that there are few national and regional policies explicitly targeting immigrant entrepreneurship in Austria. Another potential explanation is that there are no explicit policies targeting immigrant entrepreneurship in Austria (Gruber & Rauhut, 2024).

Bulgaria does not have any policies to stimulate immigrant entrepreneurship. As it is a transit country for migrants, and very few stay in Bulgaria, few policies target immigrant integration in Bulgaria. However, there are successful immigrant entrepreneurs in Bulgaria, but they have managed by themselves (Iliev, 2017; Tcholakova, 2012). In Finland, the local Chamber of Commerce and the local entrepreneurs' associations offer mentoring and advice to entrepreneurs, but there is no explicit policy or support to immigrant entrepreneurs in Finland (Davydova-Minguet et al., 2021). Although every fourth new company in Germany is founded by an immigrant, immigrant entrepreneurship is not a prioritised policy area in Germany (Metzger, 2020). Due to the governance structure in Germany, with both federal and *Länder* level, divergent, fragmented, and inconsistent processes on immigrant entrepreneurship are observable (Přívara & Rievajová, 2019).

Italy has launched several policies to stimulate a higher degree of self-sufficiency among immigrants both at national and local levels. These policies aim at providing the potential entrepreneur with a first orientation and information on entrepreneurship and then provide training courses and advice in drafting of the business plan (Bona et al., 2021). Norway has no explicit policies to stimulate immigrant entrepreneurship (Røhnebæk et al., 2021), nor has Spain (Lardiés & del Olmo, 2021).

The situation in the UK appears the same, but the country has a special visa category for entrepreneurs. This is designated for entrepreneurs from outside the EEA who wish to establish or manage a business in the UK. They must have a minimum of £50,000 in investment funds and sufficient personal savings to support themselves during their stay in the UK (Caputo & Baglioni, 2021). While immigrant entrepreneurs face challenges such as navigating the visa system and accessing funding, there are initiatives and policies in place to support them. For instance, the UK's AI Opportunities Action Plan includes proposals to attract and retain top talent in sectors like AI and life sciences (Dheer, 2018).

7.4 A Swedish 'Sonderweg'?

To comprehend the contemporary development of immigrant entrepreneurship in Sweden, it is essential to examine its historical evolution. While contemporary immigrant entrepreneurship in Sweden exhibits numerous similarities, but also differences, with that in other countries, one must ask whether Sweden historically displayed such parallels with other countries. Since the nineteenth century, Sweden has had a light-hearted attitude towards immigrant entrepreneurs, preferring labour immigration (Nordlund, 1999). While many of Sweden's competitors try to attract competence and entrepreneurs, Sweden still today does the opposite: highly skilled and entrepreneurs are deported (or not granted visa) with reference to murky arguments about the labour market regulations (Rauhut et al., 2023). Instead, Sweden has experienced an increase in low-skilled immigrants who are unable to provide for themselves (Eklund & Larsson, 2023). Without employment, being included in the Swedish social insurance system is difficult (Carlson & Hatti, 2016). A modest estimate indicates that share of this group almost counts for 15 percent of the population in working age in Sweden (Eklund & Larsson, 2023). Self-employment has become a policy measure to put these people into work; the aim is not how these people can stimulate the Swedish economy (Andersson Joona, 2016; Hjerm, 2004). To what extent the Swedish attitude towards immigrant entrepreneurs be considered a 'Sonderweg' is an interesting question. A 'Sonderweg' refers to a societal evolution, often related to the modernisation process, considering a country to have followed a historical development unlike any other in Europe (Iggers, 2005).

During the early Middle Ages, several important institutions emerged to facilitate international trade and commerce: (1) different contractual arrangements came into use, (2) banks dealing with deposits became common, (3) it became possible to sign insurance lines for commodities, and (4) the institutions related to credits developed, which facilitated business. Much of this depended on trust of the single merchant. Since a significant share of the trade was run by Germans in the Hanseatic network, Italians in the Italian city-states and Belgians and Dutch in the Flanders, importing entrepreneurs and businessmen from these countries made it simpler to get linked up to these trading networks (North & Thomas, 1973; Cipolla, 1988). Furthermore, they were all Christians, sharing the same moral values on what was just, right, and fair in business (Rosenberg & Birdzell Jr, 1986). Importing entrepreneurs, craftsmen, and merchants was a simple tool for countries to use to get connected to these international networks as were most countries in Europe at that time (Dillard, 1967). During the Middle Ages, Sweden was linked up to the Hanseatic network (Lindkvist & Ågren, 1985).

The mercantilist policy is characterised by extensive state regulation of and state participation in economic life. In general, statesmen and monarchs doubted the merchants' loyalty. Synchronously, merchants and trading houses were important sources of funding for the state's military and political activities. One of the foundations of mercantilism was that the balance of trade should be positive, i.e. exports would exceed imports, and that a series of protectionist trade barriers were introduced against other countries. The state often took the initiative for larger industrial projects. In this context, it was important to have a diligent and skilled workforce. The monarch could grant merchants monopolistic concessions in domestic and foreign trade, protection from foreign competition, and laws that could grant exemption from taxation or increased profits. Despite these privileges, it was still the monarch who profited from this kind of policy (Dillard, 1967). In accordance with the mercantilist ideals, the Swedish state during the seventeenth and eighteenth centuries strove for the largest possible export, economic growth, and self-sufficiency. To achieve this, Sweden encouraged capital-rich foreigners to conduct their business from Sweden to increase Sweden's income. Sweden offered, among other things, tax freedom, monopolies, and concessions. At the end of the eighteenth century, however, the state stopped attracting foreign entrepreneurs to Sweden and instead began to impose restrictions on their activities (Nordlund, 1999). The Swedish Navigation Act, i.e. a regulation that limited the number of foreign ships in Swedish ports was abolished in the middle of the nineteenth century (Berend & Ranki, 1982). Concurrently, the Business Freedom Ordinance of 1864 was introduced, which limited the opportunities for foreigners to conduct business in Sweden. Instead, an immigration of skilled labour was prioritised (Nordlund, 1999). The general development in Sweden did not display any major difference to the development in other countries in the European periphery at this time (Berend & Ranki, 1982).

During the industrial revolution, huge amounts of labour needed to be transferred from agriculture to the expanding industrial sector in the towns and cities. In peripheral Europe, many people also left their native country to build up a new life abroad. North America was the prime destination for emigrants from Northern, Central and Eastern Europe, while many emigrants from Southern Europe also left for South America. In the peripheral European countries labour was needed, and especially skilled labour, to fill the vacancies in the expanding industrial sector (Kenwood & Lougheed, 1989; Berend & Ranki, 1982). From the mid-nineteenth century until the early 1930s, Sweden was a country of emigration. As a labour shortage existed, labour needed to be replaced by technological solutions. This intensive industrial expansion however required a significant accumulation of capital before the investments could be made (Schön, 2000). In Sweden, as in most other European periphery, the state was one actor with the capacity to accumulate the needed capital. The result was large-scale industrial and infrastructural investments with state involvement (Berend & Ranki, 1982). Single foreigners (craftsmen, merchants and entrepreneurs) played a marginal role here, simply because they could not accumulate the needed money for these investments. The emergence of limited liability companies, in which foreigners could be a part of, were able to accumulate the required capital (Kenwood & Lougheed, 1989; see also Jörberg, 1988; Nordlund, 1999). Moreover, foreign direct investments also reduced the significance of importing entrepreneurs (Nordlund, 1989). In that respect, it is perhaps not surprising that Sweden focused on attracting skilled labour rather than entrepreneurs.

Arguably, the situation for immigrant entrepreneurship is similar after World War II. Small businesses run by immigrants played a marginal role when huge capital was needed to rebuild Europe after the war. In many countries, only the state had the capacity to accumulate the needed capital, and this was usually made by taking credits. The size of the workforce had also been reduced due to the casualties the war had taken, which meant that labour was in desperate need in many countries. For understandable reasons, entrepreneurship was not given the highest priority politically. Still today, most advanced industrial countries compete for the STEM-workers (science, technology, engineering, and mathematics) using different visa systems to attract them (Chiswick, 2019). Other countries use tax regimes to attract e.g., entrepreneurs, professionals, and highly skilled individuals. Portugal's special tax regime for Non-Habitual Residency (NHR) offers reduced rates of tax on Portuguese-source income, while most foreign-source income is exempt from Portuguese taxation, for a period of ten years (IMI, 2023). Since 2008, Sweden offers entrepreneurs who want to start business in Sweden visa. Most visas have been granted to people from Middle East and Africa who generally start companies in industry related to unqualified service sector jobs (Kazlou & Urban, 2023).

Starting up companies that are competitive at a global level, and this is the aim of most politicians in most countries, requires accumulated capital for investment as well as human capital. No single entrepreneur possesses this, immigrant or not. Starting small business for provision of daily services and goods at a local level is important for all residents and companies nearby, but it is a too low level for the state to get involved in. These services and goods are up to single entrepreneurs to provide and finance, immigrants or not. To issue visas for starting up business providing unqualified service sector jobs will however not stimulate the economic development in a country, nor will it provide a living for the entrepreneurs. Kazlou & Urban (2023, p. 103) come to a similar conclusion when saying 'immigrant entrepreneurship often becomes a form of precarious self-employment; therefore, powerful correctives are needed to avoid overexploitation of immigrants via entrepreneurship'.

The conclusion is that the development of immigrant entrepreneurship in Sweden can hardly be considered to represent any 'Sonderweg'. On the contrary, Sweden appears to follow a similar development to other countries with small and open economies through history, and the current trajectories of immigrant entrepreneurship—a means to make a living for mainly refugees—can be traced back to the mid-nineteenth century.

7.5 Concluding Remarks

When summarising the research and scholarship on immigrant entrepreneurship in various countries and comparing the findings with Sweden, several conclusions can be drawn. One notable observation is that fewer theoretical approaches are employed in Sweden compared to international research on immigrant entrepreneurship. The reasons for this discrepancy remain unclear.

There are, however, several similarities between Sweden and other countries in this field of research. Immigrant entrepreneurship tends to flourish in sectors that require little startup capital, are labour-intensive, and have low productivity. Examples include restaurants, cafés, cleaning services, hairdressers and barbers, grocery stores, construction, and transport services. Additionally, immigrant entrepreneurship predominantly occurs in larger cities. It does not typically drive innovation but excels in market and product development, which is often mistakenly perceived as innovation. Like many other countries, Sweden does not have specific policies aimed at stimulating immigrant entrepreneurship. Existing policies generally promote entrepreneurship as a whole.

Lastly, when considering whether the development of immigrant entrepreneurship in Sweden represents a 'Sonderweg' compared to other European countries, the conclusion is no. Immigrant entrepreneurship in Sweden, along with the research conducted on it, appears to follow general trends observed in other European countries.

References

Aliaga-Isla, R., & Rialp, A. (2013). Systematic review of immigrant entrepreneurship literature: Previous findings and ways forward. *Entrepreneurship & Regional Development, 25*(9–10), 819–844.

Andersson Joona, P. (2016). Integrationspolitiska insatser för nyanlända: Vilken roll spelar egenföretagandet? In J. Eklund (Ed.), *Swedish Economic Forum Report 2016: Immigration, ekonomisk integration och entreprenörskap* (pp. 54–73). Entreprenörskapsforum.

Berend, I. T., & Ranki, G. (1982). *The European periphery and industrialization 1780–1914*. Akadémiai Kiadó.

Blumenthal, V., & Lund, P. O. (2021). Norway. In M. L. Caputo, et al. (Eds.), *10 country reports on economic impact* (pp. 194–218). MATILDE Deliverable 4.3. https://doi.org/10.5281/zenodo.5017813

Bona, M., Membretti, A., & Tonelli, D. (2021, January). Italy. In S. Baglioni, M. L. Caputo, J. Laine, & A. Membretti (Eds.), *The impact of social and economic policies on migrants in Europe* (pp. 189–232). MATILDE Deliverable 3.1 and 4.1. https://doi.org/10.5281/zenodo.4483950

Caputo, M. L., & Baglioni, S. (2021, January). United Kingdom. In S. Baglioni, M. L. Caputo, J. Laine, & A. Membretti (Eds.), *The impact of social and economic policies on migrants in Europe* (pp. 380–420). MATILDE Deliverable 3.1 and 4.1. https://doi.org/10.5281/zenodo.4483950

Carlson, B., & Hatti, N. (2016). The Swedish welfare state model: A brief overview. *Social Science Spectrum, 2*(4), 216–229.

Chiswick, B. R. (2019). Managing immigration in the 21st century. In B. Elsner (Ed.), *Foundations of migration economics* (pp. 583–595). Oxford University Press.

Cipolla, C. M. (1988). *Before the industrial revolution.* Routledge.

Davydova-Minguet, O., Havukainen, L., Laine, J., & Pöllänen, P. (2021, January). Finland. In S. Baglioni, M. L. Caputo, J. Laine, & A. Membretti (Eds.), *The impact of social and economic policies on migrants in Europe* (pp. 110–148). MATILDE Deliverable 3.1 and 4.1. https://doi.org/10.5281/zenodo.4483950

Dheer, R. J. S. (2018). Entrepreneurship by immigrants: A review of existing literature and directions for future research. *International Entrepreneurship and Management Journal, 14*(3), 555–614.

Dillard, D. (1967). *Economic development of the North Atlantic Community.* Prentice-Hall.

Dudi, V., Del Baldo, M., & Gabriella Baldarelli, M. (2021). A structured literature review of immigrant entrepreneurship. Insights from Italy. In C. Bevilacqua, F. Calabrò, & L. Della Spina (Eds.), *New metropolitan perspectives* (pp. 844–858). Springer.

Eklund, J. E., & Larsson, J. P. (2023). *Det nya utanförskapet.* Ekerlids förlag.

Flikkema, M., Jansen, P., & Van Der Sluis, L. (2007). Identifying Neo-Schumpeterian innovation in service firms: A conceptual essay with a novel classification. *Economics of Innovation and New Technology, 16*(7), 541–558.

Gruber, M., & Rauhut, D. (2024). *Immigrant entrepreneurship beyond the cities in Austria and Sweden: A policy analysis.* A paper presented at the 63rd European Regional Science Association's Congress, 26–30 August 2024 in Terceira Island, Azores, Portugal.

Hjerm, M. (2004). Immigrant entrepreneurship in the Swedish Welfare State. *Sociology, 38*(4), 739–756.

Hyams-Ssekasi, D., & Chimenya, A. (2024). The theoretical perspective of migrant entrepreneurship in the United Kingdom. In D. Hyams-Ssekasi & E. Daskalaki (Eds.), *Migration and entrepreneurship in the global context* (pp. 3–23). Palgrave.

Iggers, G. G. (2005). *Historiography.* Wesleyan University Press.

Iliev, S. (2017). *Where there is a will, there is a way. Private sector engagement in the employment of beneficiaries of international protection.* UNHCR. Retrieved September 16, 2024, from https://www.unhcr.org/bg/wp-content/uploads/sites/18/2019/03/CATRO-Employment-Report-EN-FINAL.pdf

IMI. (2023). *Pivoting for prosperity in Portugal: Post-NHR tax benefits for innovators.* Accessed December 19, 2023, from https://www.imidaily.com/sponsored-feature/pivoting-for-prosperity-in-portugal-post-nhr-tax-benefits-for-innovators/

Jörberg, L. (1988). *Svenska företagare under industrialismens genombrott 1870–1885.* Lund University Press.

Kazlou, A., & Urban, S. (2023). Swedish migration policy liberalization and new immigrant entrepreneurs. *International Migration, 61*(2), 87–106.

Kenwood, A. G., & Lougheed, A. L. (1989). *The growth of the international economy 1820–1980.* Unwin Hyman.

Kordel, S., & Weidinger, T. (2021). Germany. In M. L. Caputo, et al. (eds.), *10 country reports on economic impact* (pp. 130–160). MATILDE Deliverable 4.3. https://doi.org/10.5281/zenodo.5017813

Kotler, P., Armstrong, G., Harris, L. C., & He, H. (2020). *Principles of marketing.* Pearson.

Krasteva, A. (2021, January). Bulgaria. In S. Baglioni, M. L. Caputo, J. Laine, & A. Membretti (Eds.), *The impact of social and economic policies on migrants in Europe* (pp. 59–88). MATILDE Deliverable 3.1 and 4.1. https://doi.org/10.5281/zenodo.4483950

Lardiés, R., & del Olmo, N. (2021, January). Spain. In S. Baglioni, M. L. Caputo, J. Laine, & A. Membretti (Eds.), *The impact of social and economic policies on migrants in Europe* (pp. 271–309). MATILDE Deliverable 3.1 and 4.1. https://doi.org/10.5281/zenodo.4483950

Levie, J. (2007). Immigration, in-migration, ethnicity and entrepreneurship in the United Kingdom. *Small Business Economics, 28*(2), 143–169.

Lindkvist, T., & Ågren, K. (1985). *Sveriges medeltid.* Norstedts.

Metzger, G. (2020). *Wieder mehr migrantische Gründungen.* KfW Research: Volkswirtschaft Kompakt 205 (11.12.2020). Retrieved September 16, 2024, from https://www.kfw.de/PDF/Download-Center/Konzernthemen/Research/PDF-Dokumente-Volkswirtschaft-Kompakt/One-Pager-2020/VK-Nr.-205-November-2020-Migrantengruendung.pdf

Naz, G. (2017). *Økt andel gründere blandt innvandrerne, Statistics Norway.* Retrieved September 17, 2024, from https://www.ssb.no/virksomheter-foretak-og-regnskap/artikler-og-publikasjoner/okt-andel-grundere-blant-innvandrerne%2D%2D327627

Nordlund, S. (1989). *Upptäckten av Sverige. Utländska direktinvesteringar i Sverige 1895–1945*. Umeå Studies in Economic History no. 12. Department of Economic History, Umeå University.

Nordlund, S. (1999). Invandrarföretagande i Sverige—En historisk tillbakablick. In Kulturdepartementet, *Invandrare som företagare*, SOU 1999:49 (pp. 354–364). Regeringskansliet.

North, D. C., & Thomas, R. P. (1973). *The rise of the Western world: A new economic history*. Cambridge University Press.

Paoloni, P., De Andreis, F., & Papa, A. (2024). Relational capital and immigrant entrepreneurship in Italy. *International Entrepreneurship and Management Journal, 20*(4), 2703–2727.

Přívara, A., & Rievajová, E. (2019). Destination marketing and policies attracting high-skilled individuals in Germany and Singapore. *Transnational Marketing Journal, 7*(2), 229–244.

Ram, M., & Jones, T. (2008). Ethnic minorities business in UK: Review of research and policy development. *Environment and Planning C: Politics and Space, 26*(2), 352–374.

Ram, M., Jones, T., & Villares-Varela, M. (2017). Migrant entrepreneurship: Reflections on research and practice. *International Small Business Journal, 35*(1), 3–18.

Rauhut, D., Pöllänen, P., Havukainen, L., Laine, J., & Davydova-Minguet, O. (2021). Finland. In M. L. Caputo et al. (Eds.), *10 country reports on economic impact* (pp. 93–129). MATILDE Deliverable 4.3. https://doi.org/10.5281/zenodo.5017813

Rauhut, D., Aigner-Walder, B., & Schomaker, R. (2023). *The economics of immigration beyond the cities: Theoretical perspectives and empirical insights*. Palgrave Macmillan.

Riesco-Sanz, A. (2008). ¿Repensar la sociología de las economías étnicas? El caso de la empresariabilidad inmigrante en Lavapiés. *Migraciones, 24*, 91–134.

Røhnebæk, M., Warhuus Samuelsen, N., & Lund, P. O. (2021, January). Norway. In S. Baglioni, M. L. Caputo, J. Laine, & A. Membretti (Eds.), *The impact of social and economic policies on migrants in Europe* (pp. 233–270). MATILDE Deliverable 3.1 and 4.1. https://doi.org/10.5281/zenodo.4483950

Rosenberg, N., & Birdzell, L. E., Jr. (1986). *How the West grew rich: The economic transformation of the industrial world*. Basic Books.

Rydvalova, P., & Skala, M. (2021). Innovation and innovation partnership. In M. Zizka & P. Rydvalova (Eds.), *Innovation and performance drivers of business clusters. Science, technology and innovation studies*. Springer. https://doi.org/10.1007/978-3-030-79907-6_4

Schön, L. (2000). *En modern svensk ekonomisk historia*. SNS förlag.

Tcholakova, A. (2012). The professional careers of refugees in Bulgaria and France. *Sociological Issues, 2012*(1–2), 256–274.

Vinogradov, E., & Isaksen, E. J. (2008). Survival of new firms owned by natives and immigrants in Norway. *Journal of Development Entrepreneurship, 13*(1), 21–38.

Vitores, M., Fernández, M., & Caro, R. (2020). Migrant entrepreneurship in Spain: A systematic review. *Revista Internacional de Estudios Migratorios, 10*, 1–39.

CHAPTER 8

Reflections and Conclusions

Abstract In this final chapter, the main findings are summarised, and their impact is reflected upon. Some remaining gaps in literature are identified and some avenues for future research are proposed. Policy implication, such as e.g., a more active support to immigrant entrepreneurs is also discussed. The added value of this study is also explicated.

Keywords Historical continuity • Institutional change • Path dependency • Policy implications

8.1 Main Findings

This essay explores immigrant entrepreneurship in Sweden through both economic and historical lenses. While the overview starts in the Middle Ages, the primary focus is on the past 60 years. The questions this chapter proposed to answer are (1) in what sectors and industry immigrant entrepreneurship has taken place, (2) why it has taken place, (3) where it has taken place geographically, and (4) what its economic and social impact have been. The chapter will also try to answer (5) to what extent the development of immigrant entrepreneurship in Sweden is unique for Sweden or has followed international trends.

Two main paths can be identified regarding the sectors and industries in which immigrant entrepreneurship has taken place. On the one hand,

D. Rauhut, *Immigrant Entrepreneurship in Sweden*, https://doi.org/10.1007/978-3-032-02466-4_8

until the mid-nineteenth century, Sweden struggled with poverty and underdevelopment and hence sought to attract ambitious foreign entrepreneurs. These foreigners were expected to bring the financial resources, networks, and knowledge that Sweden lacked. Many of these foreigners were already well-off when they arrived in Sweden. By the mid-nineteenth century, the financial capacity of individual foreign merchants was insufficient to start and operate companies; these merchants simply could not accumulate the capital needed when industrialisation in Sweden began. Instead, limited liability companies, which could be owned by foreigners and were not discriminated against, replaced them. On the other hand, throughout the entire investigated period, artisans, craftsmen, and shop-owners of foreign origin have run their businesses in Sweden. During some periods, they have encountered institutional discrimination (e.g., the 1864 Business Freedom Ordinance) or racism, which e.g., Jews have experienced intermittently throughout history.

The answer to the second question on why immigrants has started companies in Sweden points in several directions. Historically, Sweden actively invited foreign entrepreneurs, with financial resources, networks, and knowledge, attracting them with tax incentives, religious freedom, special legal privileges, and, notably, monopolistic concessions that guaranteed profits. This generosity stemmed from Sweden's significant shortages in knowledge, capital, networks, and other resources. During this period, immigrant entrepreneurship was intended to *supplement* the lack of domestic entrepreneurship in certain sectors and industries. However, it was not only resource-rich merchants who came to Sweden, but also ordinary e.g., artisans, craftsmen, and shop-owners. To what extent these immigrant entrepreneurs enjoyed the same privileges as the resource-rich merchants before the introduction of the 1864 Business Freedom Ordinance is unknown. What we do know is that the introduction of the Business Freedom Ordinance of 1864 altered the landscape of immigrant entrepreneurship. This ordinance was discriminatory against immigrants wishing to start *small* businesses, although it did not prevent them from owning and operating joint-stock companies or partnerships with Swedish partners. Small-scale immigrant businesses were prohibited from competing with domestic enterprises in the same industry. While the ordinance was in effect, small-scale immigrant entrepreneurship served as a *complement* to domestic entrepreneurship.

Immigrant entrepreneurship expanded significantly after the repeal of the Business Freedom Ordinance in the late 1960s. Initially, Europeans were the primary founders of businesses in Sweden, but by 1990, one in four small businesses was operated by a Third Country National. This increase in immigrant entrepreneurship correlated with the growing difficulties, particularly for non-European immigrants and refugees, in securing employment in the regular labour market. The 2010s saw a significant influx of refugees from Africa and Asia, who struggled with labour market integration and formed ethnic enclaves in metropolitan areas. Within these enclaves, some immigrants became entrepreneurs, providing goods and services to their communities. Immigrant entrepreneurship typically concentrated in low-productivity, labour-intensive sectors with slim profit margins, such as restaurants, taxis, hairdressers, convenience stores, retail, cleaning companies, and personal services. Consequently, immigrant entrepreneurship emerged as a *parallel* phenomenon to native entrepreneurship, rather than a supplementary or complementary one. Refugee entrepreneurs primarily serve their compatriots within ethnic enclaves, operating independently of the broader domestic entrepreneurial landscape. Contemporary immigrant entrepreneurs have not been invited to Sweden, nor are they offered tax incentives or monopolistic concessions. Most of them engage in entrepreneurship with the hope of securing their livelihood.

The third question addressed where geographically immigrants have started their companies. Immigrant entrepreneurship has historically been an urban phenomenon. It has consistently targeted economically significant cities across various historical periods. In a sparsely populated country like Sweden, both historically and presently, the market for goods and products was concentrated in urban areas where consumers could be found, thereby generating the aggregate demand necessary for business profitability. Some immigrant entrepreneurs produced goods for the international market, situating their operations near essential natural resources. Despite production occurring outside urban centres, the business owners typically resided in economically significant cities of the respective historical periods. Notably, Stockholm and Gothenburg were home to the majority of these entrepreneurs.

What the economic and social impacts were of immigrant entrepreneurship was addressed in the fourth question. The relative economic impact of immigrant entrepreneurship was historically more significant than it is today. This is an interesting observation. Historically, invited immigrants introduced new ideas, technologies, products, and services to Sweden, a country then deficient in financial resources, knowledge, and skilled labour. These entrepreneurs were granted tax breaks, monopolistic concessions, and legal freedoms to facilitate their contributions. These immigrant entrepreneurs typically hailed from affluent merchant families and were well-connected politically, representing an economic upper class. If Sweden were to invite contemporary entrepreneurs such as Bill Gates, Jeff Bezos, and Elon Musk to establish their businesses in the country today, offering them similar incentives, they would likely succeed. However, these individuals would not be representative of the general immigrant entrepreneurs in Sweden, who often struggle to sustain family businesses or self-employment.

The social consequences of immigrant entrepreneurship in Sweden can be examined from various perspectives, particularly focusing on how well these entrepreneurs assimilated or integrated into Swedish society. Immigrant entrepreneurs arrived in Sweden through different means: some were invited to set up businesses, while others came as labourers or refugees and later started businesses. The integration of foreign entrepreneurs during the Middle Ages is not well-documented, but conflicts with native entrepreneurs were noted (Heckscher, 1963). Significant immigration from England, Scotland, Wallonia, the German countries and the Netherlands occurred in the seventeenth and eighteenth centuries, with many immigrants being Protestant, which likely facilitated their integration (Svanberg & Tydén, 1992). In the mid-nineteenth century, the nature of immigration shifted, with many Jewish refugees fleeing pogroms in Russia (including present-day Poland, Lithuania, and Ukraine) coming to Sweden (Nordlund, 1999). Despite earlier invitations to Jewish entrepreneurs, discrimination persisted until after World War II.

After World War II, labour immigrants and refugees from Nordic countries were seen as brothers, while those from Germany were treated as guests. Refugees from the Baltic countries, Poland, Russia, and Jews were regarded as parasites and treated accordingly (Byström, 2006). Many of these groups lived secluded lives in Sweden, separate from the rest of the population (Rauhut, 2014). The integration of refugees was poor during this period, but the small number of refugees meant that increasing segregation was not seen as a problem (Rauhut, 2019). From 1957 to 1981, the reliance on social assistance among immigrants in Sweden rose sharply, particularly affecting immigrant men who had previously worked in heavy industry, which was now being rationalised due to increased international competition (Broström & Rauhut, 2018). In the new Millennium, 'immigrant entrepreneurship often becomes a form of precarious self-employment; therefore, powerful correctives are needed to avoid overexploitation of immigrants via entrepreneurship' (Kazlou & Urban, 2023, p. 103).

To what extent the development seen in Sweden is unique compared to other countries is investigated in the fifth question. The short answer is no. Sweden appears to follow the development of many other small countries with open economies, situated in the European periphery. In broad terms, the conducted research in Sweden on immigrant entrepreneurship addresses the same issues as are raised in the international research, using the same theories and approaches.

8.2 Immigrants, Entrepreneurship and Institutional Change

The industrial breakthrough in Sweden in the late nineteenth century was facilitated by deliberate policies enacted by the Swedish state. Without the complex interplay between the state as an actor and the business sector, an industrial revolution would not have occurred. The state consciously utilised its economic power to bolster its own position, both domestically and in international competition. Industrialisation was not driven solely by market forces; rather, the Swedish state played an active role in this process. The state contributed to the removal of outdated laws and regulations, but to describe the institutional changes that took place during the 1840s and 1860s as a period of deregulation is misleading. Instead, it was a period of re-regulation, during which a more contemporary institutional framework was established (Magnusson, 2005). This applies to entrepreneurship in general and, consequently, to immigrant entrepreneurship as well.

According to Marxist theory, capitalism develops through a series of historical and economic transformations. Capitalism emerged when the productive forces (such as technology and labour) advanced during industrialisation, rendering the feudal system inefficient. This led to the development of capitalist production relations (capital owners and wage labourer) and a capitalist superstructure (such as contractual freedom and competition) (Sweezy, 1970). Capital accumulation, according to Marx (1981), occurs as capitalists invest in means of production (such as factories and machinery) and employ workers to produce goods. Workers receive wages for their labour, but the value of what they produce exceeds their wages. This difference, which Marx termed *surplus value*, accrues to the capitalists and is reinvested in production to generate even more capital.

The Business Freedom Ordinance of 1864 should be seen from this context: it was introduced to facilitate capital accumulation during the industrial take-off period. The corporate form sole proprietorship was insufficient to accumulate capital, and hence it was discriminated against. The conclusion is that the de facto discrimination against immigrant entrepreneurship by the Business Freedom Ordinance of 1864 was a side-effect, not the main aim.

Institutional economic theory explains the emergence of capitalism by focusing on the role of institutions in economic development. According to this theory, institutions are the rules, norms, and organisations that structure human interaction and economic activity (North, 1999; North & Thomas, 1973; Rosenberg & Birdzell Jr, 1986). North (1999) argues that economic growth and the rise of capitalism depend on effective institutions that protect property rights, enforce contracts, and reduce transaction costs. These institutions create a stable environment where investment and innovation can flourish, leading to capital accumulation and economic growth. Rosenberg and Birdzell Jr (1986) also emphasise the importance of technological change and innovation, driven by institutional frameworks that promote research and development. By creating incentives for entrepreneurship and technological advancement, institutions contribute to shaping the dynamics and growth of capitalism.

From an institutional economics perspective, the introduction of the Business Freedom Ordinance of 1864 appears to serve the purpose of establishing effective institutions that protect property rights, enforce contracts, and reduce transaction costs. Such institutions, in turn, create a stable environment conducive to investment and innovation, thereby fostering capital accumulation and economic growth. This has been touched upon in previous research (see Jörberg, 1988; Arlebäck, 1996). During the industrialisation process, the corporate form of sole proprietorship became insufficient in this context, as economies of scale increased in significance. Again, the discrimination against immigrant entrepreneurship by the Business Freedom Ordinance of 1864 appears a side-effect.

Sweden's EU membership altered the conditions for entrepreneurship in many ways. The free movement of goods, services, capital, and labour within the EU not only simplifies trade and business operations but also expands a market where the same conditions as in the home country apply. Labour that is a citizen of an EU country does not need to apply for work and residence permits to work in another EU country (CEC, 2014; in 't Veld, 2019). EU membership also means that a citizen of an EU country can start and run a business under the same conditions as the country's own citizens (Barnard, 2013). Overall, Sweden's entry into the EU represented a significant institutional change, with a substantial impact on the conditions for entrepreneurship. While EU citizens who established companies in Sweden became privileged immigrant entrepreneurs, as they were afforded the same status as natives, non-EU immigrant entrepreneurs remained disadvantaged, as they continued to be classified as immigrants. Moreover, it is worth remembering that the abolishment of the old national regulations when Sweden entered the EU does not mean deregulation; rather, it means that another set of regulations have replaced the old ones.

8.3 Critical Junctures

Several significant institutional changes occurred in the mid-nineteenth century. For example, in 1846, unmarried women were granted the same rights as men to start and run businesses, and the first limited liability company law was introduced in 1848 (Magnusson, 2002). The guild system was abolished in 1846, and the credit market was deregulated and expanded. Additionally, several crucial markets, particularly those related to forestry, mining, and iron ore production, were deregulated in the early 1840s. Export customs on industrial products were also lifted during this period (Schön, 2000). Different customs rates between foreign and Swedish ships were abolished in 1857 (Magnusson, 2005). The timber and sawmill industries boomed 1830–1860, and by the economic expansion in these sectors, they paved the way for the industrialisation of Sweden in the 1890s (Jörberg, 1965).

In 1864, the Business Freedom Ordinance was introduced, which broadly liberalised business activities (Schön, 2000). However, it discriminated against sole proprietorships and particularly affected immigrants who sought to establish smaller businesses. The period from the 1840s to the 1860s represents a time of rapid and significant institutional change in entrepreneurship in Sweden. Consequently, this period must be considered a critical juncture for immigrant entrepreneurship.

The 1864 Business Freedom Ordinance was finally repealed in the late 1960s, marking the beginning of a new period of rapid institutional change in Sweden. This period culminated with Sweden's accession to the

European Union in 1995. Following Sweden's entry into the EU, the institutional framework for immigrant entrepreneurship underwent fundamental changes. EU citizens residing in another EU Member State were no longer considered immigrants; only non-EU citizens retained this designation. Consequently, EU citizens residing in another Member State acquired the same legal status as native citizens.

The period from the late 1960s to the mid-1990s represents a critical juncture in the history of immigrant entrepreneurship in Sweden, characterised by significant institutional transformations. Nordlund (1999) asserts that the period surrounding World War II constitutes a critical juncture and that the epochs preceding and following the war represent distinct eras in his periodisation. This assertion, however, has not been substantiated in this essay.

8.4 Looking Onwards and Outwards

This essay has highlighted several areas that require further exploration. One such area pertains to refugees and entrepreneurship. In the late nineteenth century, visible minorities, particularly refugees and Jews from the Russian Empire, encountered substantial barriers to entering the Swedish labour market. For these groups, entrepreneurship often represented the sole viable means of livelihood. However, the Business Freedom Ordinance of 1864 imposed restrictions, making it challenging for them to establish businesses unless they acquired Swedish citizenship or partnered with Swedish nationals (Svanberg & Tydén, 1992). Today, many refugees arrive uninvited and start small enterprises as a means to escape unemployment (see Chap. 3). *For the past 150 years, self-employment and the establishment of small businesses have consistently served as crucial strategies for refugees to overcome unemployment and sustain their livelihoods in Sweden.* Most of them start businesses in low-productive and labour-intensive sectors, which are characterised by low profitability and high risks of financial insolvency. From this perspective, it is necessary to discuss whether entrepreneurship is the best way to utilise the labour supply offered by these refugees.

Moreover, while much is known about immigrant entrepreneurs hailing from affluent merchant families, who were politically well-connected and represented an economic upper class, little is known about the conditions experienced by artisans and craftsmen who came to Sweden as immigrant entrepreneurs to start small businesses. The knowledge gap is most concerning for the period between the Middle Ages and the introduction of the 1864 Business Freedom Ordinance. The privileges offered to affluent merchant families moving to Sweden resemble those offered to multinational corporations (e.g., Google and Amazon) starting operations in Sweden, such as tax breaks and subsidies for almost everything. Immigrant entrepreneurs starting small businesses receive no such privileges. Although no previous research has highlighted this so far, it seems doubtful that immigrant entrepreneurs of small businesses historically enjoyed the same privileges as the affluent and politically well-connected merchants moving their businesses to Sweden. This is an area that future research should investigate.

Another area for future research to explore is the definition of an immigrant entrepreneur. Sole proprietorships, partnerships, and smaller limited liability companies can be defined as immigrant enterprises depending on who asserts ownership and control over the company. In larger limited liability companies, it is difficult to identify the owner and who controls the company, as the shareholders can be numerous, making it challenging to determine if it is an immigrant company or not. The 1864 Business Freedom Ordinance discriminated against sole proprietorships, which significantly impacted immigrants who wanted to start companies; limited liability companies were not discriminated against, and this corporate form allowed foreigners to own and control companies in Sweden. The problem of identifying immigrant entrepreneurship is not new. Without a scientifically sound discussion on what constitutes immigrant entrepreneurship and who qualifies as an immigrant entrepreneur, the terms immigrant entrepreneur and immigrant entrepreneurship will become synonymous with refugee entrepreneurship in the forms of sole proprietorships, partnerships, and smaller limited liability companies. In times when issues related to refugees' difficulties in establishing themselves in the labour market and the costs of receiving refugees are associated with negative sentiments, there is a risk that such entrepreneurship will receive less support and be deprioritised on the political agenda.

A key avenue for future research is the examination of macro-level institutional shifts in relation to the lived experiences and strategic adaptations of immigrant entrepreneurs. To what extent have these experiences and strategies evolved over time, and how have they been shaped by whether immigrant entrepreneurship functions as a supplement, complement, or parallel to Swedish entrepreneurial activity? While this research area represents a significant gap in existing scholarship, it nonetheless holds considerable potential for advancing our understanding of the factors that drive immigrants towards entrepreneurship. However, it is also crucial to interrogate whether the conceptual distinction between 'supplement', 'complement', and 'parallel' captures the full complexity of immigrant entrepreneurial trajectories, or if alternative frameworks might offer more nuanced insights into their economic and social positioning within Sweden's business landscape.

Institutions determine immigrant entrepreneurship by shaping the legal, economic, and social environment in which businesses operate. By understanding and addressing these institutional factors, policymakers can create more supportive conditions for immigrant entrepreneurs, fostering economic growth and social integration. One area in which institutions affect immigrant entrepreneurship is through legal and regulatory frameworks. Regulations that require citizenship or partnerships with nationals can limit opportunities for immigrants (Dheer, 2018). This essay has explicated that the Business Freedom Ordinance of 1864 in Sweden can either facilitate or hinder immigrant entrepreneurship. Policies that provide or restrict access to work visas, residency permits, and citizenship can significantly impact an immigrant's ability to start and sustain a business (Vandor, 2021). Historically, the regulation that banned Catholics and Jews from entering Sweden effectively reduced their capacity to start and run companies in Sweden. Today's 'entrepreneurship visas', however, mainly attract asylum seekers whose applications have been rejected, facilitating immigrants' ability to start companies in Sweden.

A second main area in which institutions affect immigrant entrepreneurship is related to economic policies. Economic policies that offer tax breaks or subsidies to businesses can encourage entrepreneurship. However, these benefits are often more accessible to larger corporations than to small immigrant-owned businesses (Chodavadia et al., 2024). Similar findings have been made in this essay's historical overview. Moreover, institutions that provide financial support, such as loans and grants, can help immigrant entrepreneurs overcome initial capital barriers. Conversely, lack of access to financial resources can be a significant obstacle (Malki et al., 2022). The findings in this essay support this conclusion.

A third area in which institutions affect immigrant entrepreneurship relates to social and cultural support. Institutions that facilitate networking through business associations, chambers of commerce, and mentorship programs can help immigrant entrepreneurs integrate into the local business community (Morales et al., 2022). As pointed out above, little is known about the conditions' immigrant entrepreneurs struggled with in older times; in contemporary Sweden, networking is facilitated at local levels. Furthermore, societal attitudes and cultural acceptance of immigrants can influence their entrepreneurial success. Supportive environments that value diversity can foster immigrant entrepreneurship, while discriminatory practices can hinder it (Dheer, 2018). The discriminatory practices targeting Jews in Sweden between the late nineteenth century and World War II are an example of the interplay between social acceptance and immigrant entrepreneurship.

Institutional embeddedness constitutes a fourth area in which institutions affect immigrant entrepreneurship. The extent to which immigrants are integrated into the economic fabric of the host country affects their entrepreneurial activities. This includes access to markets, resources, and business networks, i.e., what is known as economic embeddedness (Muñoz-Mora et al., 2022). Immigrants' integration into the social and cultural life of the host country can impact their business ventures. Institutions that promote social inclusion and cultural diversity can enhance entrepreneurial opportunities. This relates to the immigrants' sociocultural embeddedness (Dheer, 2018). The institutional embeddedness of immigrants in Sweden is probably key to understanding why some immigrants succeed in the regular labour market, while others become entrepreneurs.

Institutions can create path dependency in immigrant entrepreneurship by establishing long-lasting frameworks and practices that shape opportunities and barriers. Understanding these institutional influences is crucial for developing policies that can break negative path dependencies and foster a more inclusive entrepreneurial environment. Institutions that historically provided or restricted access to financial resources, markets, and networks can create persistent advantages or disadvantages for immigrant entrepreneurs. For example, if certain groups have historically been excluded from financial support, this can create ongoing barriers. The degree to which immigrants are integrated into the economic fabric of the host country can create a path-dependent trajectory. Those who have established networks and resources are more likely to succeed, reinforcing existing patterns. The extent to which immigrants are integrated into the social and cultural life of the host country can influence their entrepreneurial opportunities. To what extent the immigrants decide to opt out from integration into the social and cultural life of the host country will have the similar impact. Institutions that promote social inclusion can create positive path dependencies, while those that do not can perpetuate exclusion. The extent to which immigrant entrepreneurship in Sweden has become path dependent is something for future research to take a closer look at.

8.5 Final Remarks

This essay on immigrant entrepreneurship, spanning several centuries and identifying both path dependencies and critical junctures, offers several significant contributions. By examining a long historical timeline, the essay reveals how immigrant entrepreneurship has evolved, highlighting enduring patterns and shifts over time. This provides a deeper understanding of the historical context and continuity of entrepreneurial practices among immigrants in contemporary Sweden. Discovering critical junctures where major changes occurred allows for the identification of pivotal moments that have shaped the trajectory of immigrant entrepreneurship. These insights can help explain how and why certain changes happened, offering valuable lessons for current and future policymaking.

By uncovering path dependencies, this essay shows how past decisions and events have influenced the present state of immigrant entrepreneurship. This can help in understanding the constraints and opportunities that have persisted over time, providing a nuanced view of the entrepreneurial landscape. The findings can inform policies aimed at supporting immigrant entrepreneurs by highlighting successful strategies and practices from the past. Understanding historical successes and failures can guide contemporary efforts to foster a more inclusive and supportive environment for immigrant entrepreneurship.

This essay enriches the academic discourse by filling gaps in the literature and providing a robust framework for future research. It can serve as a foundational reference for scholars interested in the intersection of immigration, entrepreneurship, and economic history. By shedding light on the contributions of immigrant entrepreneurs over centuries, the findings in this essay can help in challenging stereotypes and promoting a more positive narrative about the role of immigrants in economic development. This book illuminates the enduring impact and transformative moments of immigrant entrepreneurship across centuries, offering invaluable insights for scholars, policymakers, and practitioners alike.

References

Arlebäck, S. O. (1996). *Från ägarmakt under ansvar till företagsledarmakt u.p.a.* Lund Studies in Economic History 4. Doktorsavhandling. Lund University Press.

Barnard, C. (2013). *Competence review: The Internal Market.* Department for Business, Innovation and Skills. Retrieved October 2, 2014, from https://assets.publishing.service.gov.uk/government/uploads/system/uploads/attachment_data/file/226863/bis-13-1064-competence-review-internal-market.pdf

Broström, L., & Rauhut, D. (2018). Poor men. On the masculinisation of poverty in Sweden 1957–1981. *Scandinavian Journal of History, 43*(3), 410–431.

Byström, M. (2006). *En broder, gäst och parasit. Uppfattningar och föreställningar om utlänningar, flyktingar och flyktingpolitik i svensk offentlig debatt 1942–1947.* PhD Thesis. Dept. of History, Stockholm University.

CEC. (2014). *The single market: The general policy framework.* Retrieved October 2, 2024, from https://web.archive.org/web/20141205063154/http://ec.europa.eu/internal_market/top_layer/index_en.htm

Chodavadia, S. A., Kerr, S. P., Kerr, W. R., & Maiden, L. J. (2024). *Immigrant entrepreneurship: New estimates and a research agenda.* NBER Working Paper 32400. https://doi.org/10.3386/w32400

Dheer, R. J. S. (2018). Entrepreneurship by immigrants: A review of existing literature and directions for future research. *International Entrepreneurship and Management Journal, 14*(3), 555–614.

Heckscher, E. F. (1963). *Svenskt arbete och liv.* Aldus.

in 't Veld, J. (2019). The economic benefits of the EU Single Market in goods and services. *Journal of Policy Modeling, 41*(5), 803–818.

Jörberg, L. (1965). Structural change and economic growth: Sweden in the 19th century. *Economy and History, 8*, 3–46.

Jörberg, L. (1988). *Svenska företagare under industrialismens genombrott 1870–1885.* Lund University Press.

Kazlou, A., & Urban, S. (2023). Swedish migration policy liberalization and new immigrant entrepreneurs. *International Migration, 61*(2), 87–106.

Magnusson, L. (2002). *Sveriges ekonomiska historia.* Prisma.

Magnusson, L. (2005). *Den synliga handen. Nation, stat och det industriella bygget.* SNS förlag.

Malki, B., Uman, T., & Pittino, D. (2022). The entrepreneurial financing of the immigrant entrepreneurs: A literature review. *Small Business Economics, 58*(3), 1337–1365.

Marx, K. (1981). *Kapitalet. Första boken.* Arkiv/Zenit.

Morales, C., Brieger, S. A., De Clercq, D., & Martin, F. J. (2022). Explaining differences in entrepreneurial activity between immigrants and natives: Moderating roles of economic, sociocultural and institutional factors. *International Journal of Entrepreneurial Behavior & Research, 28*(6), 1609–1630.

Muñoz-Mora, J. C., Aparicio, S., Martinez-Moya, D., & Urbano, D. (2022). From immigrants to local entrepreneurs: Understanding the effects of migration on entrepreneurship in a highly informal country. *International Journal of Entrepreneurial Behavior & Research, 28*(9), 78–103.

Nordlund, S. (1999). Invandrarföretagande i Sverige—En historisk tillbakablick. In Kulturdepartementet, *Invandrare som företagare*, SOU 1999:49 (pp. 354–364). Regeringskansliet.

North, D. C. (1999). *Institutions, institutional change and economic performance*. Cambridge University Press.

North, D. C., & Thomas, R. P. (1973). *The rise of the Western world: A new economic history*. Cambridge University Press.

Rauhut, D. (2014). *I moder Sveas ömma famn*. Carlsons bokförlag.

Rauhut, D. (2019). Sverige, invandrarna och integrationen 1947–1967. In D. Rauhut & L. Broström (red.), *Med öppna armar? Om integration och invandring till Sverige 1945–1970* (pp. 141–162). Daidalos.

Rosenberg, N., & Birdzell, L. E., Jr. (1986). *How the West grew rich: The economic transformation of the industrial world*. Basic Books.

Schön, L. (2000). *En modern svensk ekonomisk historia*. SNS förlag.

Svanberg, I., & Tydén, M. (1992). *Tusen år av invandring*. Gidlunds bokförlag.

Sweezy, P. M. (1970). *Teorin för den kapitalistiska utvecklingen*. Rabén & Sjögren.

Vandor, P. (2021). *Why immigrants are more likely to become entrepreneurs*. Retrieved October 4, 2024, from https://hbr.org/2021/08/research-why-immigrants-are-more-likely-to-become-entrepreneurs

Index[1]

[1] Note: Page numbers followed by 'n' refer to notes.

D. Rauhut, *Immigrant Entrepreneurship in Sweden*,
https://doi.org/10.1007/978-3-032-02466-4

FSC
www.fsc.org
MIX
Papier | Fördert gute Waldnutzung
FSC® C083411

Kolibri 360 GmbH
Ferdinand-Jühlke-Straße 7
99095 Erfurt, Deutschland
produktsicherheit@kolibri360.de